The Terri Schiavo Case

The Julie Rubenzer Case

Donald W. Ayer

Donald W. Ayer

Published by Book Publishers INK

Library of Congress Cataloging-in-Publication Data:

Donald W. Ayer
The Terri Schiavo Case: The Julie Rubenzer Case

Dedication

I will dedicate this manuscript to my wife of 61 years.

"You are the best thing that ever happened to me. Julie's disaster and death is the worst thing that ever happened to us."

And to our daughter Colleen Kopshinsky who flew to Sarasota 4 times during those 10 weeks we were trapped there. And that she devoted much time in creating the diary that lead to this publication.

And to our son Wade Ayer for devoting time and money attempting to convince lawmakers to create a Cameras in Surgery. "Julie Ayer Rubenzer" via his web site "National Organization for Medical Malpractice Victims." And for the national video document "Never Events." And in addition, "writing bills that would rewrite or undo Tort Reform & raise the medical law suit caps to $3,000,000 so that a family can financially take care of themselves for the rest of their lives.

Don Ayer

Acknowledgment

1.Maureen Ayer, Julie's mother. She was less than enthusiastic about publishing this over 20 year old document, but she did not object. Otherwise, this record would not exist.

2. Babette Bach, Sarasota Guardianship attorney who saved my guardianship in circuit Court.

3. Larry Bonet. Julie's 4 month boyfriend who upon being told that we, Julie's family, intended to remove life support, called me a murderer.

4. Sarasota County Sgt. Chris Iorio. who happened to be at the right place at the right time. When he heard Bonet's threat to me placed me under police protection all the way to Wisconsin.

5. Sarasota County States Attorney Office who deemed her malpractice death as. "Accidental."

6. Atty. Bob Jackson, Bonet's atty who screamed that he is "Gonna call the Legislature and force those parents to fly her from Wis. back to Sarasota."

7. Dr. Kurt Dangl, her cosmetic surgeon, who delivered

1650 mgs. Propofol.

8. And to the RUG we pulled out from under the Religious Rightists, Larry Bonet. Bob Jackson, Johnny Byrd, and Gov

Jeb Bush.

Contents

About the Author

Don Ayer resides in Waukesha, Wisconsin, with his wife of 61 years, in the same home where they raised their three children—Colleen, Julie, and Wade.

A 1962 graduate of the University of Wisconsin-Platteville, Don holds a Bachelor's degree in English and Journalism. His professional journey began with 15 years as a life insurance salesman, during which he adhered to the suit-and-tie corporate world. Following that, he transitioned into real estate, a field in which he remains active to this day.

The account you are about to read is a true story. It is told with minimal embellishment—no unnecessary adjectives or adverbs. What transpired was life-altering. Faced with overwhelming grief and anger, we had to devise a way to manage both, simultaneously.

I found myself needing to think, speak, and act like a big-city trial lawyer—an entirely new way of life. The cooperation and support of my family, especially my wife Maureen, were essential. Together, we managed through 10 intense weeks, followed by a lifetime of enduring those changes.

So, before you proceed, I advise you to fasten your seatbelt.

Introduction

For those born between 1990 and 2024, the name Terri Schiavo may not be familiar, as the media coverage surrounding her case largely subsided by 2005. However, individuals from the previous generation—parents or grandparents—will likely recall the significant national attention it received. From 1995 to 2005, the case was a regular feature in the news, dominating headlines throughout the day.

The Florida House and Senate even passed a special law, known as "Terri's Law," which granted Governor Jeb Bush the authority to intervene on behalf of Schiavo's parents. This intervention sought to remove guardianship from her husband, Michael Schiavo, in an effort to prevent him from discontinuing her life support. It arguably became one of the longest-running news stories in U.S. history, with the case escalating over a decade through various judicial bodies, including Circuit Court, the Florida Supreme Court, federal courts, and even the U.S. Supreme Court. The matter also drew attention from the Vatican and other influential institutions.

In contrast, the case of Julie Rubenzer, which ran from September 2003 to December 7, 2003, in Sarasota, Florida, was much shorter in duration—just 10 weeks compared to the 10-year legal battle in Schiavo's case. Both women were in a persistent vegetative state (coma), but the outcomes and public reactions were markedly different. Michael Schiavo faced intense criticism, with some from the religious right labeling him a murderer. Similarly, I, as Julie's father and legal guardian, was subjected to the same accusations. Ultimately, those who opposed us in these cases were unsuccessful.

So, why am I revisiting this case after 20 years? In October 2003, when we met with our guardianship attorney, Babette Bach, she advised us to document the unfolding events. My wife, Maureen, diligently maintained a journal through December 30, 2003, keeping a comprehensive record.

This past summer (2024), I found myself reflecting on these events and decided to search for any recent updates on the Schiavo case. I came across two books: Terri: The Truth by Michael Schiavo and Michael Hirsh, and Using Terri by Jon Eisenberg. Both of these works were a revelation to me, offering insights that renewed my understanding of the privacy invasions we endured at the hands of the religious right. They reminded me of how personal matters can become the subject of public debate, and how these debates persist even two decades later.

Now, I have decided to share our story and the records we kept. We narrowly avoided becoming a second "Terri Schiavo case" by a mere day. For further context, I encourage anyone unfamiliar with the case to look up the Terri Schiavo story and its significance.

Chapter One

The grief of a parent is unlike any other. There is a natural order to life—children are meant to outlive their parents. But when that order is shattered, when a child is lost, it's as if the very fabric of life is torn apart. It's a sorrow so profound that no words can truly capture its depth. As parents, we spend our lives nurturing, protecting, and guiding our children, hoping to shield them from harm. But when the unthinkable happens, when we are powerless to save them, it leaves an emptiness that nothing can fill.

It was on such a path of heartbreak that Maureen and I found ourselves in the fall of 2003. Our daughter, Julie, was vibrant, beautiful, and full of life. She was the second of our three children, born on January 29, 1965. We never imagined that our world, once full of light and laughter, would be plunged into darkness.

September 25, 2003

It was a Thursday afternoon, and I was wandering through a home supply store, browsing for a stovepipe for our new lake property in northern Wisconsin. Maureen and I had recently bought the place and had been working tirelessly to turn it into a retreat, a sanctuary for us and our family. Life had been good. We were at the top of the world, looking forward to a visit from Julie, who lived in Sarasota, Florida.

Then, my phone rang, shattering that peace forever. It was Maureen, her voice trembling. "Don, you must come home!" she said, panic creeping into her words. When I pressed her for an explanation, she could barely get the words out: "Julie went in for a breast implant this morning, and now they can't wake her up."

I felt the ground shift beneath me. Time slowed. The world that had been so steady just moments ago was now crumbling. I rushed home to find Maureen, grief-stricken and terrified. She kept repeating, "They can't wake her up!" I could see the fear in her eyes. We had been through something like this before—Colleen's father-in-law had fallen into a coma two years prior and never woke up. We knew all too well what those words could mean.

Desperate for answers, we called Julie's ex-husband, Bob Rubenzer, who knew nothing of the surgery. Even her close friend Tina Valente was blindsided, unaware that Julie had gone under the knife. Julie had kept her surgery a secret, knowing her friends would have disapproved.

In the chaos, Maureen and I asked ourselves, "What do we do? Should we fly to Florida?" After confirming the severity of the situation with Julie's boyfriend, Larry Bonet, we quickly booked the first flight we could find.

September 26, 2003

The next morning, Colleen drove us to the airport. The sky was a dull gray, mirroring the weight of dread that pressed upon us. As we flew toward Sarasota, my mind drifted through memories of Julie's life. She had been a star from the moment she was born, lighting up every room she entered, effortlessly drawing people to her with her natural beauty and vivacious personality.

We arrived in Sarasota by mid-morning, but nothing could prepare us for what we would face. The hospital was a sterile, cold place, and yet, it now held all of our hope and fear. We prayed for some miracle, for our Julie to open her eyes and smile, but deep down, the dread had taken root.

The Weight of Memories

As I sat in that waiting room, I couldn't help but let my mind wander back to Julie's childhood. Born in Lansing,

Michigan, we moved to Madison, Wisconsin, when she was just two years old. Despite the upheavals of several moves, Julie adapted with grace. She was always the center of attention, from her time in middle school when boys followed her everywhere, to her high school years when she became a cheerleader and won a bikini contest during Spring Break.

Julie's life was full of moments of joy, excitement, and laughter. She was a force of nature, the kind of person who never experienced a dull moment. And while her beauty drew people to her, it was her vibrant personality that made her unforgettable.

But now, as I waited for news that seemed to never come, I wondered how this had all gone so wrong. How had we gone from watching Julie grow into this dynamic woman to sitting helplessly in a hospital, praying for her to wake up?

Sarasota, and the Life We Didn't Know

The move to Sarasota in 2001 had seemed like a new chapter in Julie's life. After her divorce from Bob, she had settled into a beautiful home in Sarasota, with an indoor pool and an idyllic lifestyle. From the outside, everything seemed perfect. But life has a way of hiding its cracks, and Julie's world was not as flawless as it appeared.

We had started to sense that things were unraveling in her marriage to Bob. Though she had seemed to love the life they built together, there were signs that all was not well. Eventually, she left Bob, filed for divorce, and began a new relationship with Larry.

Still, we never imagined it would end like this. We were in Sarasota now, but it felt as though we were trapped in some terrible dream. The vibrant girl who had lit up every room was lying in a hospital bed, unresponsive. We were powerless, clinging to hope even as we feared the worst.

I'll never forget the day a nurse pulled me aside into a janitorial closet. She was visibly nervous and quickly pulled out a pen. "You didn't get this from me," she warned. "If you did, I would never be able to work in the medical field again. They can't explain who gave what, how much, or when. Their timelines are off, erased, and rewritten." She handed me a piece of paper and said, "You better get yourself a good attorney." On that piece of paper, she had written one word: Propofol.

After that conversation, I went downstairs to the lobby where I found my son, Wade, and we stepped outside to talk. It was in that moment that I realized I had been pulled into a code of silence—a veil of secrecy surrounding the medical mishandling of my daughter's case.

Years later, the state's attorney confirmed what I had long suspected. "Mr. Ayer," he told me, "you see what's happening here. They're all in on it. The surgeons cover for each other, and the American Medical Association (AMA) knows it. The hospital associations and insurance companies do too. You're far ahead of yourself on this, but you need to reach out to your state legislators and congressmen."

I followed that advice and reached out to them, but my efforts were met with indifference. The legislators, including Tyler Vorpagel, Glen Grothman, Devin LeMahieu, and Ron Johnson, all turned a blind eye. They are part of what I call the "do-nothing club"—people who hear no evil and see no evil, so they don't have to do anything about it.

However, there was one exception. State Representative Christine Sinicki actually listened. She took my concerns seriously and helped put bills in motion to address the issues we were facing.

October 6, 2003

Days passed in a blur of hospital visits, updates from doctors, and prayers that felt like they were falling on deaf ears. We watched Julie, our vibrant, beautiful daughter, fading away before our eyes.

Julie left a void that nothing could ever fill. It was a kind of pain that goes beyond tears, beyond words. Our daughter was gone, taken from us far too soon, and we were left to pick up the pieces of a life that had been so full of promise.

I'll never forget the day we had to fly her out of Florida under a police escort. It was one of those situations you never imagine happening to your own family, but life can be unpredictable like that. Larry, Julie's boyfriend, had become volatile, and things had escalated to a point where he threatened my life. I can still recall the tension in the air, the worry etched on all of our faces, and the uncertainty about what might happen next.

The situation with Larry had been difficult for some time, but when someone makes a direct threat to your safety, especially from someone who once was part of your family's life, it shakes you. It's an experience that leaves a mark, not just because of the danger, but because of the emotional toll it takes on everyone involved.

We knew we couldn't take any chances. Julie's safety, and the safety of our family, came first. That's when Sheriffs Sgt. Chris, suddenly became involved in our case. Chris was someone we could trust, and his support during that time meant more than I can express. He arranged for a police escort to ensure that Julie could leave Florida safely, with no interference from Larry. It was an extraordinary measure, but it was necessary given the circumstances.

The day we flew her out was tense. We had coordinated everything carefully, and Chris and his team were with us every step of the way. I remember the relief I felt once we were finally at the airport, but there was still that nagging worry until the moment the plane took off. Until then, it felt like anything could happen.

I'm still in contact with Chris to this day, and if anyone ever questioned the events of that time, he can verify what happened. It was a difficult chapter in all of our lives, one I wouldn't wish on anyone. But having the right people around us—people like Chris who were willing to go above and beyond to protect our family—made all the difference.

What struck me most throughout that ordeal was the strength Maureen showed. Despite everything, despite the fear and the tension, she remained composed. She trusted that we were doing everything we could to keep her safe, and she showed remarkable courage in a situation that could have easily broken anyone's spirit.

We never imagined we would find ourselves in a situation like this, where a threat to our family would come from someone we had once known. But it taught me something valuable: when it comes to protecting the ones you love, you do whatever it takes. I would have done anything to keep Julie safe, and in that moment, I realized just how far we'd go for our family.

After we got Julie out of Florida, things slowly began to settle. We had to take certain precautions, of course, and we remained vigilant for a while, but the immediate danger had passed. Larry's threats didn't materialize into further action, and we were able to put some distance between that part of our lives and move forward.

In retrospect, I realize how fortunate we were to have the support we did. People like Chris, who acted not just as a professional but as someone who genuinely cared about our well-being, made all the difference. It's a reminder that in times of crisis, the strength of your community, the people who stand by you, is what really carries you through.

It was a dark time for our family, but we came out the other side stronger. Maureen's resilience, the unwavering support of those around us, and the knowledge that we did everything we could to protect each other are what I remember most about that difficult chapter in our lives. It wasn't easy, but we made it through—together.

As parents, we had always tried to protect our children, but in this moment, we were utterly helpless. All we could do was hold onto each other and remember the light that Julie had brought into our lives—the memories of a girl who had lived life with passion, joy, and a sense of adventure that few could match.

In her absence, we clung to the words she had once written on her kitchen chalkboard: "Life is good." Those words were her motto, and they would become our way of remembering her spirit. Even in our darkest moments, we would try to find some light, because that is what Julie would have wanted. But life, without her, would never be the same again.

As the days in Sarasota dragged on, our hope began to waver. We clung to the optimistic words of the nurses, who assured us that there was still a chance Julie might wake up, but the longer she remained unresponsive, the more we started preparing ourselves for the worst. Conversations among us were punctuated by long silences, the weight of uncertainty pressing heavily on all of us.

Bonet's behavior grew more erratic. He fluctuated between bouts of helpfulness and strange outbursts. On the one hand, he showed concern for Julie's condition and invited us to stay at his home, but on the other, his paranoia was increasing. He began acting as though we were intruding on his life rather than being there for our daughter. This erratic behavior only fueled our growing distrust, especially after he brought up the idea of selling Julie's cars. Wade was particularly suspicious, convinced that something was off, but none of us could place exactly what it was.

Then came the MRI results, and our tenuous hope took another blow. Dr. H, the pulmonologist, delivered the news with a clinical detachment, explaining Julie's vegetative state in cold medical terms. I knew in that moment that this wasn't going to end with Julie walking out of the hospital like her friends so naively believed. The image of my daughter, vibrant and full of life just weeks ago, contrasted sharply with the medical prognosis we were facing.

Wade and Colleen, ever practical, decided we needed to regain control over the situation. We realized that if we didn't act swiftly, we could lose everything—from Julie's financial assets to her medical decisions. The idea of Bonet having any kind of control over Julie's life was unfathomable to us, and we were determined to prevent that from happening.

So, the next morning, Wade and I made arrangements to meet with a local guardianship attorney. Maureen stayed at the hospital with Colleen, unwilling to leave Julie's side for even a moment. In that sterile office, surrounded by stacks of legal papers, I felt like we were about to go into battle— not just against the system, but against the chaos that Julie's life had become in the past few months. As the attorney outlined the steps to secure temporary guardianship, the reality of the situation sank in deeper. We were fighting for control of our daughter's future, both legally and financially, but we were also coming to grips with the fact that we might never get the Julie we knew back.

Back at the hospital, Bonet's behavior continued to deteriorate. When I returned that afternoon, he was standing outside the ICU, pacing and muttering angrily into his phone. I couldn't make out the words, but the tension in his body was obvious. When he saw me, his eyes flicked with something between suspicion and anger. He quickly ended his call and approached me.

"I need to talk to you," he said, his voice low but agitated.

"About what?" I asked, already feeling my stomach tighten.

"About this whole situation—Julie's money, her cars, her house. We need to be practical here. You're her parents, but we were about to get married. I should have a say in what happens next."

It was the first time he'd directly implied that he should have some control over Julie's estate, and it sent a chill down my spine. I could feel Wade's words from earlier that day echoing in my mind—something isn't right with Bonet.

"We're handling it," I said, trying to keep my voice steady. "Right now, our focus is on Julie's health, not her assets."

He scoffed, shaking his head. "You don't understand. Julie and I had plans. She trusted me with everything."

I stepped back, putting distance between us. "I think we need to have a serious talk about what's going to happen from here, but now's not the time."

Bonet's expression hardened. "You're pushing me out, aren't you? Just because I'm not her husband yet doesn't mean I don't care about her."

"You've known her for a few months, Larry," I said quietly. "We've known her for 38 years. We're her family."

The conversation ended there, but I could see the tension building in him. I knew this wasn't the last we'd hear from Bonet on the subject of Julie's finances. We were all exhausted, emotionally drained from the ongoing uncertainty, but now we had to add Bonet's unpredictable behavior into the mix. The weight of everything felt unbearable, and I realized we were not only fighting for Julie's life but for control over what was left of it.

The following morning, after another sleepless night, Maureen, Colleen, and I returned to the hospital, hoping for some small improvement in Julie's condition. But there was nothing new. Julie remained as she had been, trapped in her own body, unable to respond to our voices or touch.

Wade, ever the pragmatist, suggested we begin going through Julie's house to gather any necessary documents—bills, financial statements, insurance policies—that could help us navigate the coming legal hurdles. Maureen and I reluctantly agreed. It felt strange, almost wrong, to be rifling through her personal belongings while she lay in a hospital bed, but we knew it had to be done.

That afternoon, we made the trip to her house on St. Armands Circle. Walking into the place she'd so proudly bought just months earlier was surreal. The house was a mix of chaos and unfinished decorating, a reflection of the turmoil that had taken over her life recently. Boxes were stacked in the hallway, half-unpacked. Papers were scattered across the dining room table, alongside magazines and mail.

Maureen stood in the middle of the living room, looking around in disbelief. "I can't believe this is her house," she said softly.

"It doesn't even feel like her," I replied.

We began sorting through her things, trying to make sense

of the mess. There were stacks of bills, contracts with decorators, notes scribbled in Julie's handwriting. But what struck me the most were the little personal items—her favorite perfume bottle still sitting on the bathroom counter, a half-finished book on the nightstand. Each small reminder of her life before this tragedy tugged at my heart.

As we went through her papers, we found what we had been looking for—her will. Maureen unfolded the document carefully, her hands trembling slightly. We read it together, and the reality of the situation hit us like a freight train. Julie's will, if it had ever been executed, left almost everything to Rubenzer's daughters. It was as if she had never considered the possibility that her parents would need to step in and handle her affairs.

It was late April, maybe early May, when my son visited Julie. She had an apartment at the time. I remember him telling me about the close call he had while walking up to her place. He said the window cleaners accidentally dropped a squeegee from about 15 floors above, and it almost hit his head. The thought of it sent chills down my spine. He could have been killed, just like that. When he told me the story, though, he joked about it, saying, "Mom and dad would have been mad!" That's just how he is—always finding humor in situations that would terrify most people.

But what struck me more than the near-miss was what Julie told him later. She confided in him that she had named him as the full beneficiary in her will. Now, I knew the bond between the two of them was strong. They shared a unique closeness that not every sibling has. But even still, hearing that she wanted everything to go to him... well, that was something.

I wasn't there when she said it to him, of course. It was one of those private moments between the two of them. But later, when we were on the way to see Bob Rubenzer to get some legal documents sorted out, my son decided to tell me what Julie had said. I was driving, and he just came out with it. He said, "Julie told me I'm the sole beneficiary in her will."

Now, I know my son. I've known him his entire life, and I've watched him grow into a man of integrity, a man who values family and loyalty above all else. I didn't need to think twice about it. I looked at him and simply said, "I'm not worried. I know you'd never do anything selfish." And that was the truth. There was no part of me that believed he'd take advantage of the situation. He's the type of person who would always do what was right, even if it wasn't the easiest choice.

I appreciated that he told me, though. He didn't want any surprises, and that's the kind of man he is—honest, upfront, and considerate of how things affect others. It's funny how, in a moment like that, I felt proud of him. Not just for how he handled the situation, but for the kind of person he had become. A father can't ask for much more than to see his children grow into people of integrity and kindness.

But life has a way of throwing curveballs, doesn't it? In the end, Julie never signed her will. For all the things she may have wanted to happen, for all the plans she might have had, they never came to pass. The will didn't become official, and when everything was said and done, her estate went to her stepchildren.

It wasn't how she had intended it, I'm sure of that. I know she had wanted to take care of her brother, and she had probably spent time thinking about how to make sure he was provided for. But when the paperwork doesn't get signed, the legal system takes over. And that's what happened.

In the end, though, my son didn't show any anger or bitterness about it. He didn't come to me upset that Julie's wishes hadn't been followed. He took it in stride, just as he does with most things. I think deep down, he knew that his relationship with Julie wasn't defined by Julie's will or her money. What they shared went far beyond that. They had a bond that was stronger than any legal document, and no matter what happened with her estate, that bond remained intact.

As her father, I felt a certain sadness that Julie's intentions weren't carried out the way she had hoped. But I also felt a sense of peace knowing that my son handled it with such grace. Life doesn't always go the way we plan, and sometimes the things we think are important—like wills and inheritances—turn out to be less significant than we imagined. What truly matters are the relationships we build, the love we share, and the way we treat each other while we're here.

Looking back, I realize that the greatest inheritance my son received from Julie wasn't financial. It was the love and connection they shared, the memories they built, and the way they supported each other through life's ups and downs. No will could have captured that, and no legal document could have measured its value.

Julie never have signed her will, but in the end, her brother didn't need it. What he had from her was far more precious than any inheritance could ever be. And as her father, I couldn't be prouder of the way they both navigated that chapter of their lives. They showed me what it means to be family, and for that, I am deeply grateful.

I felt a sinking feeling in my stomach. We were in for a legal battle, not just with the medical side of things but with her estate as well. There was no way Bonet would simply step aside now, especially not with what we had discovered. The gravity of it all weighed heavily on us, but we were determined to fight for our daughter, no matter what it took.

As the sun began to set, casting long shadows across the living room, we gathered the important papers and locked up the house. It was time to return to the hospital and face another long, uncertain night. But now, more than ever, we knew we had to be ready for whatever was coming next.

October 7, 2003

Maureen and I stood outside the ICU once again,

gathering our thoughts. The weight of making a decision about the trachea tube pressed heavily on us. We had no illusions about what this meant for Julie's future. Installing the trachea tube would likely prolong her life, but what kind of life? The doctors were clear about the odds—a less than 10% chance of recovery to any semblance of a "quality life." But Julie had always been so vibrant, so full of energy, that it was hard to reconcile that image with her current state. How could she live like this?

We knew we had to act. As Julie's guardians, Maureen and I had the authority, but more than that, we had the responsibility. The last thing Julie would ever want was to be kept alive by machines, unable to move or communicate, reduced to something far less than herself. But at the same time, this was our Julie—our sister, our daughter—and the thought of letting her go felt impossible.

Later that day, Maureen and I gathered with the rest of the family—Wade, Colleen, Mom, and Dad. We sat around the small waiting room, a few words exchanged here and there, but mostly silence. Everyone knew what was coming, though no one wanted to say it out loud. The doctors had already prepared us for this moment, and we had discussed it in bits and pieces, but now it was time for a decision.

"We all know what Julie would want," Maureen finally said, breaking the silence. Her voice was soft but resolute. "She told us. She wouldn't want to live like this."

There were murmurs of agreement. Wade, always the most emotional of us, nodded, his eyes rimmed with tears. "She told me once, too. No machines. She'd hate this."

Colleen looked at Mom, who sat quietly, staring at her hands. "What do you think, Mom?" she asked gently.

Mom took a deep breath. "I think... I think Julie would want us to let her go. She was never one to be still, to be tied down. This... this isn't her."

We all knew it was true. Julie's life had always been about movement, excitement, adventure. She thrived on new experiences, on being with people, on the next big thing. The idea of her trapped in a body that no longer worked, her mind dulled or gone, was unbearable.

We made the decision together, in that small room, without much fanfare. The doctors had given us options, but in the end, it came down to what we knew in our hearts: Julie wouldn't want this. We told the medical team to withhold the trachea tube.

That night, I sat by Julie's bedside, holding her hand. Machines beeped softly in the background, and her chest rose and fell with the rhythm of the ventilator. Her face was peaceful, but her stillness was haunting. I thought about all the times we had laughed, fought, and shared secrets. How she had always been there for me, through thick and thin. And now, she was slipping away, and there was nothing I could do to stop it.

I squeezed her hand, hoping somewhere deep inside, she could feel it. "We're doing the right thing, Jules," I whispered. "I hope you know that. I hope you understand."

October 8, 2003

The next morning, the doctors began the process of withdrawing life support. It was surreal, watching the machines that had kept her alive begin to power down, the slow reduction in their mechanical rhythms. We stood by her side, each of us taking turns holding her hand, speaking to her softly, though we knew she couldn't hear us. It felt like a final vigil, a quiet farewell.

By mid-afternoon, Julie's breathing slowed. Her heart

rate dropped. The nurses and doctors were kind, compassionate, explaining each step as gently as they could. But their words faded into the background as we focused on Julie, our sister, our daughter, our friend.

We flew her on a Wisconsin (medical) Lear Jet that December. Julie died on December 26th.

The room was quiet, save for the soft sobs of our family. It felt like the end of an era, the closing of a chapter none of us were ready to let go of. But Julie was at peace now, no longer trapped in a body that couldn't keep up with her spirit.

In the days that followed, we began the process of arranging her memorial, sorting through her belongings, and trying to piece together what life would look like without her. There were still legal matters to deal with, property to recover from Bonet, and a trust to manage for Rubenzer's daughters. But for now, we allowed ourselves to grieve, to remember Julie as she had been: vibrant, full of life, always ready for the next adventure.

As we gathered as a family to say our final goodbyes, I couldn't help but think of something Julie had once said to me, during one of our late-night conversations: "Life's too short to live it standing still." Even in death, she had refused to be held in place, choosing instead to move forward into whatever came next.

But we could not and did not lift life support, YET!!

Chapter Two

September 25, 2003

Life, as I had known it, turned upside down. What once seemed so secure—our family, our daily routines, our future—suddenly teetered on the edge of an unfathomable abyss. It's remarkable how quickly things can fall apart. You spend your whole life building a foundation, and in a single moment, everything comes crashing down, as if fate itself has decided to test your limits. Philosophers speak of the fragility of life, but it's not until you're standing on the precipice of losing what you hold dearest that you truly understand what that means.

October 7, 2003

After Julie's surgery, the hospital room had become our second home. Julie lay there, motionless, breathing only because machines willed her lungs to inflate. Every day, we sat by her bedside, waiting for something—anything—to change. But each passing day felt heavier than the last, filled with the suffocating weight of despair.

Mary Vasquez, Julie's case manager at Doctors Hospital,

had been a steady presence. She tried to explain the situation to us, as if understanding the technicalities of Julie's condition could somehow make the reality less painful. Advanced Directives, she called it. I had heard the term before, but I had never really thought about it. Who does, until they're forced to?

The idea of a Living Will felt so final. A legal document that outlines your wishes in case something irreversible happens. Maureen and I had never had those conversations with Julie. Who imagines discussing the possibility of their vibrant daughter falling into a coma?

Vasquez tried to explain it all. The medical staff had reached a point where difficult decisions had to be made—decisions about ventilators, tracheostomies, and long-term care. Decisions that Maureen and I never imagined we would have to face. We were at a fork in the road, she said. Julie's life, our lives, would never be the same.

October 8, 2003

The doctors made it clear: the trachea tube was necessary. Julie had been on a ventilator through an endotracheostomy for too long. It was time to make the airway more stable if we were in this for the "long haul." That phrase echoed in my mind, reverberating with a cruel sense of permanence. We had entered a realm where time stretched endlessly, yet stood still.

During the consultation, the doctors spoke to us about quality of life—or the lack thereof. Julie's brain had suffered severe hypoxia, a condition where the brain is starved of oxygen. She was unlikely to recover. In medical terms, they called it a persistent vegetative state, a phrase that chilled me to the bone. The legal definition was clear: Julie was not coming back to us.

Yet, as her father, I could not give up. How do you resign yourself to that kind of certainty? How do you accept that the person you raised, watched grow, and loved with all your heart is now a shell of who they once were?

October 9, 2003

We gave the order for the tracheostomy. Maureen and I sat with Julie that night, trying to find the words to tell her what we were about to do. Even though the doctors assured us she couldn't hear or understand, we needed to say it out loud. We told her we were going to remove her life support, in accordance with the wishes she had expressed years before. I could barely get the words out, and Maureen cried silently beside me.

It was the hardest thing we had ever done. You never imagine having to make a decision like that for your own child. How could I? She was my little girl, and here I was, essentially telling her that it was okay for her to leave us. But she was already gone, wasn't she? That's what the doctors kept saying, but in my heart, I couldn't accept it.

October 10, 2003

We spoke with Julie's attending physician, Dr. Davinder Bhamber. He was kind, but his words were clinical. He agreed with our decision. There was nothing more they could do. We had to prepare for the inevitable. It felt like the walls were closing in on us.

But not everyone agreed. Julie's friends in Sarasota were devastated. Two of them burst into the waiting room, sobbing uncontrollably, begging us not to let her go. They felt powerless, as did we. It was heartbreaking to see the people Julie loved so broken. We all were.

Julie's fiancé, Larry Bonet, was another matter altogether.

He refused to accept what the doctors were telling us. Each time we shared a medical report with him, he would twist it into something optimistic, some distant hope that Julie was recovering. He clung to that hope so fiercely, it hurt to watch. It wasn't based in reality, but I understood why he needed it. He wasn't ready to let go. None of us were.

October 12, 2003

Bonet became increasingly desperate. He started talking about hyperbaric chamber treatments, something used to treat divers with decompression sickness. The doctors dismissed it outright—there was no medical evidence to support that it could help Julie. Her brain was damaged beyond repair. But Larry wouldn't hear it. He was grasping at straws, searching for anything that could bring her back.

He even brought in a friend who had been in a coma and made a full recovery. But Julie's situation was different. This friend had suffered a concussion, not hypoxia. Concussions heal. Brain cells that die from lack of oxygen do not.

Despite everything, Bonet clung to his belief that she would wake up. I envied him for it, in a way. It must have been easier to believe in miracles than to accept the cruel reality we were facing.

October 14, 2003

Hospitals, in their desperation to offer something—anything—also introduced us to the concept of healing touch. It sounded absurd to me. The idea that touching someone could influence their "energy field" and promote healing? It felt like voodoo, but Maureen and I allowed it. What harm could it do?

Vasquez described it as sending unconditional love to Julie, for whatever was in her highest good. I didn't believe it would work, but I watched. And for the first time in days, Julie's body seemed to relax. Her fever eased slightly, and the seizures stopped momentarily. It wasn't a miracle, but it was something.

Still, none of this changed the reality we were facing. Each day, Julie remained unresponsive. And each day, the weight of the decision we had to make grew heavier. We were running out of options, out of time, and most painfully, out of hope.

As I sat beside Julie that night, listening to the steady hum of the machines keeping her alive, I couldn't shake the feeling that we were nearing the end. I wanted to believe in Bonet's hope, in healing touch, in some sort of divine intervention that would bring her back to us. But deep down, I knew. This was the life we had been handed now, a life where we had to let go.

Our world had changed forever, and there was no going back.

In one of our conversations, Nelson told me a story I would never forget—about a gravestone in Sarasota marked in a way that showed a woman had been scalped by Native Americans. Somehow, amidst the tragedy, his stories gave me a strange sense of peace, even though my thoughts were consumed by Julie's condition.

We were anxious about Julie's progress, or lack thereof. Her neurologist, Dr. Daniel Stein, had been vague about her chances, always asking for "more time." How much time was enough? During one meeting, he finally gave us something concrete: he said he needed two more weeks before making a full assessment. That was the first time we had a deadline. He even said that if things didn't improve, he'd recommend hospice care. Maureen and I accepted the timeline. Two more weeks to see if there was any hope. Two weeks before we had to face the possibility that we might lose our girl for good.

While we were focused on Julie's condition, an unexpected legal battle was brewing. Our attorney, Babette Bach, called with unsettling news: Julie's ex-boyfriend, Larry Bonet, had hired an attorney, Robert A. Jackson, to challenge our guardianship. I was furious. As Julie's parents, Maureen and I were her legal guardians. How could Larry have any say in this? Julie wasn't married; she had no children. Bach explained that he was using something called "Interested Person" status to challenge us. He was claiming that Julie wouldn't want her life support ended, and he was willing to fight us for control over her care.

It was like being hit with another bomb. While we were struggling to make sense of Julie's medical situation, we now had to fight a legal battle just to retain our rights as her parents.

Colleen, our other daughter, flew in with her husband, Jim, to support us. We met with Bach right away. She needed an affidavit from Colleen, outlining Julie's wishes regarding life support. Bach explained that once a motion was filed, a hearing would be required within 72 hours. It felt like we were racing against time in every possible way. Bach proposed holding an informal conference with Bonet and Jackson in an attempt to defuse the situation before it escalated to court.

Later that evening, I ran into Larry at the hospital. His words cut deep. He accused us of trying to kill Julie, saying he'd spend every cent he had to stop us. The hope that we could get him on the same page with us evaporated. Any chance of unity was gone in that ICU waiting room.

October 8, 2003

The next morning, we gathered in Bach's conference room. Jackson opened by stating that Bonet and Julie had been planning to marry and that Bonet deserved a say in her healthcare decisions. Bonet himself remained silent throughout the meeting. Then, Colleen and Jim shared the story of Jim's father, who had gone into a coma after a botched knee surgery and never recovered. Their experience mirrored ours in many ways, and we hoped it would make Bonet see reason.

Bach pleaded with Jackson to withdraw the motion, telling him that we weren't even thinking about discontinuing life support for another two weeks. She also expressed our deep desire to keep Julie's situation out of the media, fearing that public attention would turn our personal tragedy into a spectacle. But there was no response from Jackson or Bonet. When I asked Bonet directly if he would accept the doctors' reports on Julie's condition, he wouldn't even look me in the eye. The silence in the room was crushing. I knew then that this battle wasn't going to end amicably.

Later that day, in the ICU waiting room, Bonet broke down. He claimed that when I returned his credit card, it was a signal that we didn't believe Julie would recover. He poured out his heart, telling me how he was losing Julie, how everyone else had someone to go home to except him. He even said he'd never find another woman. I tried to talk sense to him, but it was clear that any attempt at rational conversation was wasted.

October 9, 2003

The next day, Jackson filed the motion, and the 72-hour countdown began. A hearing was scheduled in the Circuit

Court of Sarasota County. Jackson's motion sought to overturn my appointment as Julie's temporary guardian and requested judicial intervention regarding her medical treatment. It was like a punch to the gut to see it in writing, especially the accusations that I was not acting in Julie's best interests. According to Jackson, I was not following Julie's desires and had no clear evidence that she would want her life support discontinued.

In response, Bach filed our objections. She pointed out that I had been legally appointed as Julie's guardian and that Larry had no standing as an "Interested Person" under Florida law. The legal jargon was overwhelming, but the message was clear: Larry was trying to take away our right to make decisions for our daughter, and we were determined to fight back.

While we were dealing with the legal turmoil, a new problem arose. A reporter from the Sarasota Herald-Tribune had gotten hold of the motion and wanted a comment. The last thing we needed was for this case to go public, especially with the ongoing Terri Schiavo case already dominating the news. I tried to explain the situation to the reporter, but eventually, we had to refer him to Bach.

It felt like we were fighting on all fronts—against time, against Larry, against the media—and all the while, Julie remained in a coma, the center of this terrible storm.

Bonet's attorney requested Julie's medical records, and we had no issue granting access. I signed the authorization, though Bonet's repeated insistence that he wanted to give "110 percent" puzzled me. What exactly does that mean? More prayers, extra medical tests? It was a phrase that left me with more questions than answers.

Dr. Stein, Julie's neurologist, suggested seeking a second opinion from a specialist not affiliated with Doctors Hospital. It seemed like a good idea, both to verify Dr. Stein's prognosis and to possibly offer Bonet a dose of reality if another doctor confirmed the bleak situation. We consulted Dr. Kimberly A. Monnell, who assessed Julie and held a meeting with us and Bonet.

Dr. Monnell's report was direct and disheartening:

- Julie showed no reactivity.
- Her MRI results didn't align with typical hypoxic injuries.
- She wasn't responsive to her surroundings.

- She had been off sedation for over a week.
- Her condition was severely encephalopathic, a rare and nearly irreversible state.
- Recovery to a meaningful level was incredibly unlikely.

After delivering the medical facts, she turned to Bonet, believing he was Julie's father, and gently suggested that it might be time to consider stopping treatment. Bonet, unwilling to accept this, asked about other possible therapies like hyperbaric oxygen treatments. Dr. Monnell was firm: "You can't treat hypoxic injury. Brain cells destroyed by lack of oxygen don't regenerate. Perhaps you should wait another five days."

No one in our family was shocked by Dr. Monnell's findings. The harsh truth had been clear to us for some time. However, Larry—true to form—seemed unmoved. He only trusted his own handpicked doctors, but without guardianship, he couldn't act on his stubborn beliefs.

Julie's health continued to decline. Her body began jerking in pain-like spasms every few seconds, her temperature spiked between four and six degrees due to brain swelling, and despite receiving physical therapy, there was no treatment that could wake her from the coma.

Julie's primary physician, Dr. Bhamber, provided a brief, grim report: "Minimal reaction to pain on the left side. Trach tube installation may be needed next week. Will reassess then."

Later that evening, Dr. Kirk Voelkner, a pulmonologist, gave us another update. He informed us that Julie's heart and lungs were incredibly strong and could sustain her life for years—but in a coma, locked in a vegetative state. His prognosis was even more bleak than Bonet's optimistic interpretation of Dr. Monnell's. While Bonet claimed there was a 5 to 10 percent chance of recovery, Voelkner corrected him, stating the chance was closer to 1 or 2 percent. He added, bluntly, that he wouldn't even consider accepting her as a transfer patient.

Bonet asked, "If I find a facility that will take her, would you oppose the move?" We replied that we wouldn't stop him, but the outlook was poor no matter where she went. Even a prestigious hospital like Johns Hopkins wouldn't do anything differently.

After Dr. Voelkner left, tension erupted in the room.

Maureen broke into tears and stormed out. Jim followed, yelling, "I hope you're happy now, Larry! The doctor said she could live for years in a coma!" The few strangers who had been sitting nearby made a quick exit, probably fearing a physical confrontation. And then it was my turn. I'd had enough. I walked up to Bonet, looked him squarely in the eyes, and said, "I hope you never sleep another night for the rest of your life." And then I said it again, louder.

The strain Bonet's interference put on our family was unbearable. We were drowning in grief, trying to accept what was happening, and yet he continued to drag us into these impossible, agonizing discussions about futile treatments.

That day wasn't entirely devoid of lighter moments, though. On a drive through Sarasota's heavy traffic, we spotted a bearded man in the back of a pickup truck. I couldn't resist rolling down the window to ask, "Hey, man, how long did it take you to grow that beard?" His gruff response—"A year"—made us laugh, but his next line, "I'm letting it grow until I can wipe my ass with it," had us in stitches. It was a small, much-needed moment of levity amid the heartbreak.

The next day, Dr. Voelkner gave a new assessment: "Tender in the right quadrant—testing required. Hypoxic brain coma remains the worst kind of coma." We knew that no matter how many tests were done or how many hypothetical questions were asked, the outcome wouldn't change. Even when Bonet again brought up the idea of steroids, Voelkner shot it down immediately. It was clear: nothing could reverse the damage.

Dr. Stein later echoed these sentiments, giving us an update on Julie's condition. "No significant changes, prognosis remains very poor. This won't go on for a long time." We had a brief discussion about hospice, nourishment withdrawal, and morphine. Dr. Stein, ever the compassionate professional, was as concerned about our emotional state as he was about Julie's physical condition.

Meanwhile, the media was starting to catch wind of our situation. With the Terri Schiavo case dominating the news just seventy miles away in Pinellas Park, the press was eager to draw parallels. That night, we watched in dismay as a news report came on with the headline: "Sarasota Woman Walks into Cosmetic Surgery Center, Does Not Walk Out." It was the last thing we wanted, especially with the intense scrutiny surrounding right-to-die cases at the time.

Despite the growing media attention, we knew in our hearts that Julie's situation was irreversible. Bonet's constant objections and delusions about her recovery were just noise at this point. We, as her family, were preparing ourselves for the inevitable.

In an effort to reassure the hospital administration and Julie's caregivers, we sent a letter to Doctors Hospital, expressing our confidence in their treatment. We wanted to make it clear that the doubts being raised were not coming from our family.

By October 12th, the medical updates continued to be bleak. Dr. Stein gave a comprehensive explanation of Julie's deteriorating condition, emphasizing that she had entered a vegetative state. He explained that the physical reactions we saw—jerking movements, posturing—were not signs of pain or awareness, but rather advanced neurological deterioration. He warned that infections, skin breakdown, and pneumonia would soon become serious risks.

Despite all of this, Bonet clung to hope, insisting that we wait 60 to 90 days before making any decisions. Dr. Stein firmly rejected this, explaining that such timeframes were only used to confirm a diagnosis of persistent vegetative state. There was no point in waiting longer.

Our family was emotionally exhausted, but we continued to push forward, trying to navigate the legal and medical labyrinth we found ourselves in. Even as Bonet's attorney moved to challenge my guardianship in court, we held onto the belief that we were doing what was best for Julie.

The days blurred together as we met with doctors, signed affidavits, and prepared for the hearing. Each new medical report only reinforced what we already knew—that our beloved Julie wasn't coming back.

Chapter Three

Looking back on the events leading up to her divorce from Bob Rubenzer is a painful reminder of how difficult relationships can be, especially when one person feels trapped and the other refuses to see the truth. I always hoped for the best for Julie—what father wouldn't? When she first married Bob, I thought he might be the one to bring her happiness, but things didn't turn out that way.

Bob always seemed a little off to me, and over time, I saw what was really going on. He was controlling. He didn't want Julie to be herself, to live her life fully. Instead, he tried to isolate her, moving her into quiet, out-of-the-way suburbs, keeping her from connecting with people, always hiding her away. Julie told us how jealous he was—how little he trusted her. I understand that Bob had been hurt before. His first wife had an affair, and maybe that scarred him. But instead of dealing with that pain, he brought it into his marriage with Julie, making her pay the price for his past.

Six months before their divorce, Julie's brother flew her up to Wisconsin, using his frequent flyer miles. That trip was a turning point. I remember talking with my son afterward, and he shared how Julie had opened up about feeling trapped. She confided that Bob had somehow "locked her down" financially, making it nearly impossible for her to leave him, even though she desperately wanted out. Bob's controlling nature extended beyond just where they lived—it affected every aspect of their life together.

During that trip to Wisconsin, they went to a restaurant called the 4th Base, near the Milwaukee Brewers' stadium. It was during this visit that Julie's frustration boiled over. She had been talking to Bob on the phone while they were at the restaurant, and the conversation shifted to something that had been weighing on her for a long time: her desire to have children. Julie wanted to start a family. She wanted to be a mother. And in that moment of frustration, she pointed at her brother and said, "If I don't have that baby, I'm out of this marriage. I can't live like this."

It was a raw, honest moment. Julie wasn't just venting; she was drawing a line in the sand. Having children was important to her, but Bob kept making excuses. He'd say he was sick, or that he couldn't perform when she was ovulating—always something. It broke my heart to hear that he was denying her something she wanted so deeply, something that should have been a joyful part of their marriage. Instead, it became another area where Bob exerted control, whether intentionally or not.

When Julie finally moved out, Bob called her brother, looking for answers. He seemed blindsided by her decision to leave, as if he couldn't understand what had gone wrong. Her brother didn't hold back—he told Bob about the conversation they'd had at the 4th Base, where Julie had clearly said that if she didn't have a child, she was done. But instead of owning up to it, instead of acknowledging his role in what had happened, Bob pushed back. He claimed that Julie didn't even want kids, which was an outright lie.

I know for a fact that wasn't true. I remember another moment from that same trip, when Bob was standing in our kitchen, talking on the phone with my wife—Julie's mother. He told her that he and Julie were going to try to have a baby, and my wife was overjoyed. She was so excited at the thought of becoming a grandmother, and we all thought it was a real possibility. For Bob to turn around later and claim that Julie didn't want children—it was infuriating. He was rewriting the truth, trying to protect himself from the reality that his actions had driven Julie away.

It was hard for me to watch all of this unfold. As a father, you want your children to be happy, to find love, and to be in relationships that bring out the best in them. But with Bob, that just wasn't the case. He held Julie back, kept her from the life she wanted, and refused to take responsibility for his role in their marriage's failure. Instead of supporting her dreams of having a family, he found excuses and twisted the narrative to suit his own needs.

Julie didn't deserve that. She deserved someone who would listen to her, respect her wishes, and build a life with her that was based on mutual love and support. Bob wasn't that person, and it took a lot of strength for Julie to finally see that and walk away. I'm proud of her for finding the courage to leave a situation that wasn't serving her, even though it was incredibly difficult. She knew what she wanted, and she wasn't willing to compromise her happiness or her future any longer.

Watching your child go through a divorce is never easy, but I stood by Julie every step of the way. I knew how much she had given to that relationship, how hard she had tried to make things work. But in the end, Bob's controlling behavior, his lies, and his refusal to take responsibility left her no choice but to move on.

Julie's decision to leave wasn't just about the children they never had—it was about reclaiming her life, her independence, and her right to be happy.

On October 15, 2003, our guardianship attorney, Babette Bach, had successfully obtained affidavits from Dr. Davider Bhamber, Julie's primary physician, and Dr. Daniel Deems, the doctor who would handle the trachea tube procedure. However, Dr. Daniel Stein, a neurologist, refused to provide one. These documents were crucial in demonstrating that, as Julie's guardian, I was adhering to medical advice meticulously. Bach, along with Colleen, Maureen, and I, made our way to the courthouse, just a short walk away. Bach exuded confidence, walking with a notable spring in her step—far more assurance than we had at that moment. On our way, she briefed us on how a preliminary hearing worked, explaining that only the attorneys and the judge would engage in the discussion. While no verbal testimony would be given, the collection of affidavits had already been presented to the court.

This hearing was held in the same courtroom where we were granted temporary guardianship, though Judge Nancy

K. Donnellan, who presided over the earlier case, was on vacation. Instead, Judge Andrew Owens would be taking the bench. As we passed through airport-like security and took the elevator to the sixth floor, we saw Julie's attorney, Sharon O'Day, had also arrived. Upon entering the courtroom, we saw Julie's fiancé of two weeks, Larry Bonet, seated with his lawyer, Robert A. "Bob" Jackson, and another man, later identified as Edwin M. Boyer, Jackson's law partner. None of them would look at us. As is customary in Sarasota County courts, a deputy sheriff stood just inside the courtroom, and a judicial assistant sat at the far front on the left. Two women occupied spectator seats, whose identities puzzled us until Bach clarified that they were nurses with an interest in the case. However, she suspected they were affiliated with a right-to-life group. Upon Bach's request, they left the courtroom.

Once the room was silent, the deputy sheriff called the court to order: "Circuit Court is now in session. All cell phones must be turned off. Honorable Judge Owens presiding. All rise." Judge Owens, a tall, bearded intellectual, entered the room and sat behind the bench. His opening statement was unexpectedly touching. He extended the court's sympathy to all involved, acknowledging that no decision would fully satisfy anyone and that words could never encompass the depth of the tragedy. Owens then addressed Jackson, Bonet's attorney, asking what relief he sought from the court. Jackson responded that the evidence would prove I should be removed as guardian, and he pressed for the appointment of a temporary guardian. He argued that Bonet, as Julie's fiancé, or an independent guardian, should be given authority over her medical decisions. He launched into a tirade, accusing me of being impulsive, lacking clear evidence of Julie's inability to recover, and painted me in the most derogatory terms imaginable, stopping just short of labeling me a murderer. Among the worst of his claims was that my negative attitude had worsened Julie's condition. This vicious attack stunned me, Colleen, and Maureen, but it was clear the primary target was me.

Jackson continued, stating that we had disregarded Bonet's rights, insisting that he should have a say in Julie's medical treatment. He then presented affidavits and letters from Bonet's friends and Julie's friends, including a statement from Robert "Bob" Rubenzer, Julie's ex-husband, who had shifted his support to Bonet. To our shock, it seemed all of Julie's Sarasota friends had turned against us. Jackson further argued that by refusing to authorize the use of a hyperbaric chamber, we were denying Julie essential life support. The most appalling revelation, however, was an affidavit from Dr. Ruan Jin Zhao, a practitioner of Oriental Medicine, who had conducted an assessment of Julie without our or the hospital's consent. This was a blatant violation of hospital policies, as only doctors with hospital privileges could evaluate patients. Yet, Zhao not only performed this unauthorized assessment but also signed an affidavit. After introducing his credentials, Zhao claimed he had visited Julie about ten days after her medical incident and, based on his observations, concluded that treatments existed that could alleviate her symptoms and improve her chances of recovery. He admitted, though, that he lacked access to her medical records and could not provide a more detailed opinion.

When Jackson finished his presentation, I felt utterly defeated as Julie's guardian. How could Bonet—after just a few months of knowing Julie—bring us, her parents, into court to challenge our guardianship? Could their brief relationship hold more weight than the 38 years we had with our daughter? Bonet had even managed to gather letters of support from his and Julie's friends. The most outrageous claim came from one of Bonet's closest friends, who accused me of wanting Julie dead for financial gain.

Next, it was our attorney's turn. Bach introduced evidence showing that I had never taken steps to withhold treatment, a milder term than what Jackson had suggested. She emphasized that Maureen and I had adhered to medical advice at every step. The reason we had hesitated to authorize the trachea tube, she explained, was to delay moving Julie from the hospital to a nursing home. Bach urged the court to judge my actions, not just my words. At one point, Judge Owens asked, "What would be wrong with appointing an independent guardian?" That question seized my attention—was Bonet really about to win? Bach stood firm, pointing out that there was no compelling evidence for my removal as guardian.

Owens, perhaps feeling conflicted, made a curious reference to another case, remarking that "Judge Greer had hair before he took over the Terri Schiavo case." He appeared to be wrestling with a dilemma. He raised questions about whether Julie had signed an organ donor card, though that was irrelevant. It became clear he was struggling with the weight of the decision. Owens eventually suggested both sides agree to an independent neurological assessment from a neurologist with impressive academic credentials who wasn't from the Sarasota area. This became the court's order.

The hearing left Maureen, Colleen, and I in a state of disbelief. Jackson had unleashed a devastating attack on our family. After leaving the courtroom, we huddled in a conference room with O'Day and Bach. Bewildered, I asked, "What just happened in there?" We all concluded that the judge had essentially punted the case back to the original judge, who had been on vacation. Bach and O'Day agreed that, with the notoriety surrounding the Schiavo case, no one wanted to handle our situation. The attorneys reassured us that the other side's case was weak and full of complaints, but O'Day aptly described the hearing as a brutal assault on my character.

Maureen's journal entry from that day summed it up: "I couldn't believe what I was hearing about Don. He and Julie were so close. It was despicable. All he wanted was for our beloved Julie to wake up and smile again." We couldn't understand how some of Julie's friends could write such cruel things about us. A lot of the statements were hastily written, full of spelling mistakes, suggesting they had been hastily composed. Some even claimed we wanted Julie dead. All we had ever wanted was for her to come back to us. That day, it became clear—we were truly alone in Florida. We had each other, but we wanted Julie. While our attorney reassured us that we hadn't lost, we also hadn't won. She predicted there would likely be an evidentiary hearing, where live testimony would be given without a jury. It seemed inevitable that we would be dragged back to court after the third neurological assessment was completed.

As this ordeal unfolded, I learned a harsh lesson. In casual conversations with Bonet and his lawyer, they were gathering information that would later be used against us in court. What seemed like offhand comments became ammunition in the legal battle. I now offer "Julie's Warning" to anyone who finds themselves in a similar situation: never engage with an adversary's attorney. They are not concerned about your well-being, no matter how they might appear. Don't make eye contact, don't fall into their trap—just never engage.

The hearing intensified our sorrow, turning it into a toxic mix of grief and rage. Bonet and his lawyer seemed unable to grasp the reality of Julie's "persistent vegetative state." In the midst of this, Wade received an email from a nurse who had chosen to remain anonymous. The nurse expressed her concern for our family, acknowledging the tremendous stress we were under. She reassured us that Julie was receiving excellent care, but also pointed out the tragic reality that Julie had become a pawn in a legal-medical game. She feared that Larry's resources would enable him to continue this relentless legal assault against us. It was a grim reality we now had to face.

October 16, 2003

The local Tampa TV station once again broadcast its cheerful greeting: "Good Day, Tampa Bay." While the atmosphere in Tampa may have been pleasant, our experience in Sarasota had been far from good. Maureen and I were informed that no evidentiary hearing would be scheduled at this time, though Bonet and his attorney retained the right to request one. Julie's doctors had inserted a PEG tube and were scheduled to place a tracheostomy tube the next day. The ultimate decision rested with us, but it was heavily guided by medical and legal counsel. With our hands tied in court, Maureen and I had little choice in the matter.

October 17, 2003

The tracheostomy tube was inserted into Julie that morning, though her condition remained unchanged. After dropping Colleen off at the airport, Maureen and I spent the rest of the day grocery shopping.

October 18, 2003

Julie's condition was stagnant, still locked in a vegetative state. Her body temperature spiked to 102 degrees, and she appeared to be in pain, grimacing frequently. While no one could definitively confirm whether she was in pain, her expressions suggested as much to us.

October 19, 2003

Maureen and I had an intense discussion with Dr. Bhambar, who was clearly frustrated to learn that Bonet had clandestinely brought in a holistic doctor for an assessment without the hospital's approval. Per hospital policy, only practitioners with privileges could evaluate or treat patients. Bhambar was further upset by the fact that this doctor had signed an affidavit regarding his observations. We also updated him on the court's order for a third neurological opinion, though we remained unaware of who would be conducting the evaluation. Since the ICU doctors had done all they could for Julie, she was transferred to a private room on the hospital's third floor.

October 20, 2003

Yet another "Good Day, Tampa Bay" blared from the television, morning and night. I had given up on trying to retrieve Julie's car title, jewelry, and clothes from Bonet, so I left that to our attorneys, Bach and O'Day, who planned to send a formal request to Bonet's lawyer. After a frustrating meeting with our attorney, Maureen became deeply distressed. She felt we were losing the case and that Larry's legal maneuvers had trapped us. "There's no end to the legal harassment," she said. "Even after the third opinion, they'll demand more." She feared we were bound to lose. In her journal, Maureen expressed feeling overwhelmed and resentful, wanting to spend time with Julie but being unable to because of the ongoing court battle. The constant news about the Schiavo case on "Good Day, Tampa Bay" didn't help matters.

Despite the overwhelming frustration, I tried to stay grounded, reminding Maureen that we hadn't lost the case; we were merely enduring the legal harassment until the court made its final decision. We could sense that the hospital staff was keeping their distance from us, likely wary of potential lawsuits from either us or Bonet. Maureen and I felt isolated in Sarasota, a city that still felt foreign to us. Nonetheless, I was confident that no court would strip us of our guardianship without irrefutable proof of our incompetence. The sooner we could push for an evidentiary hearing, the better. But for now, we had to endure the daily delays, frustrations, and legal harassment.

We were constantly told by concerned friends, "He can't do that," to which I would respond, "Oh yes, he can—and he did." Our attorneys had advised us not to interfere with Bonet's visitation rights, so every day we found ourselves entering Julie's room as Bonet left, and vice versa—a silent, emotionally charged "changing of the guard." This ongoing lifestyle was unbearable. Maureen's health was deteriorating; she wasn't eating properly and was losing weight. I too had lost weight, and hip pain had forced me to stop my long-standing running routine after 22 years. I did join the Sarasota YMCA for a month, unsure how long we'd remain here.

In her journal, Maureen reflected on the small comforts that kept us going—the constant letters and cards from friends and family in Wisconsin, which became our emotional lifeline. We displayed them all over the house, reminders of the wonderful support we had from back home. Yet, the reality was stark: Bonet had trapped us in court proceedings, and we had no idea how long it would continue. We still held guardianship, but every decision we made was scrutinized by the court. Even though our choices were based on sound medical advice, this legal interference felt like an encroachment on our parental rights, even though we understood those rights had technically expired when Julie turned 18.

Maureen and I agreed that, for our own sanity, we needed to establish some kind of routine. So our days began at 7 a.m. with coffee, a walk to St. Armands Circle for a newspaper, some TV news, then a drive to Doctors Hospital. Over time, we stopped spending long hours at Julie's bedside. She didn't know we were there, so we limited our visits to about an hour in the morning and another in the afternoon, alternating with Bonet's visits. Our evenings were spent walking around St. Armands Circle, watching TV, and trying to push away the constant feelings of sorrow and anger.

October 21, 2003

Julie had been in a coma for a month now, and her condition was slowly worsening. The previous week, Attorney Sharon O'Day had suggested we explore a medical malpractice suit against Dr. Kurt Dangl, the plastic surgeon responsible for Julie's care on that tragic day in September. We met with O'Day and two other lawyers, Richard Filson and Cynthia Barry, to discuss the case. Filson, a quick thinker, explained that in most cases, there is a valid defense, but he saw none here. He believed we had a strong case, though Florida's recent legislation imposed caps on malpractice awards. While Florida law did not allow parents to sue for the loss of an adult child, because I was Julie's guardian, I could file the lawsuit on her behalf.

Filson advised us not to dwell too much on the suit's outcome—it was unpredictable. We chose to let the lawsuit proceed and focus on the present. Maureen and I weren't sure if we had chosen the right lawyer for such a case, but Filson's drive and motivation reassured us for the time being.

October 27, 2003 — Another Blow

I arrived at the hospital around 10 a.m. that day. Julie's blood count had dropped alarmingly low, prompting the doctors to arrange for a transfusion. Bonet, wanting to speak with me in private, led me outside the hospital entrance. He began by discussing the duration Julie had been deprived of oxygen during surgery under Dr. Dangl's care. Dr. Dangl had told him it was two minutes, but Bonet seemed taken aback when I revealed that it had been longer than that. None of us truly knew the precise number of minutes.

Bonet then shifted gears, confiding in me that he had consulted his attorney over the weekend. According to his lawyer, neither Maureen nor I could sue Dr. Dangl as Julie's parents; only a spouse or child could take legal action. Though I already knew this, I stayed silent, concealing the fact that I had already filed a lawsuit on Julie's behalf. Then came the real shocker—Bonet asked me to sign documents, as Julie's legal guardian, allowing him to marry her. That way, he could sue Dr. Dangl. His suggestion left me utterly speechless. I had never encountered a more repulsive proposal. Compared to this, the attack by his attorney seemed trivial. I firmly told him I would never sign such a document and insisted that if Julie were ever to marry, it would be of her own free will. As he walked away, he muttered, "Well, she was going to marry me." I was left wondering if he truly believed he could marry her while she was in a coma. I later learned that, in some rare and exceptional cases, courts do permit marriage if a couple has been cohabitating for a significant period, especially when one partner stands to gain financially. Despite what I had heard, the whole idea seemed far-fetched.

Preparing for the evidentiary hearing was a complex and costly affair. Though it was a trial without a jury, it was still a trial, and I knew it would be a brutal one. Everyone would be attacking each other from all sides. The hearing was scheduled for Wednesday. While driving to Tampa Airport to pick up Colleen, who was flying in for the hearing, Maureen stayed by Julie's side. Later that day, one of Julie's friends, Lynn, arrived with two other individuals.

Despite a clear sign on the door that read "NO

VISITORS," they walked in. Only clergy and Bonet had been allowed in previously; we didn't want anyone sneaking in with cameras or other potential disruptions. Julie would have despised the idea of anyone seeing her in that state. Lynn asked Maureen if Julie was still in a coma since her eyes were open. The other couple, apparently from California, began examining her medications and medical equipment as though they were assessing her condition. When Maureen inquired if they were conducting a medical examination, Lynn responded that they were not, but both were doctors. She added that they had vacationed with Julie in Jamaica earlier that year. Maureen quickly reassured them that Julie had excellent doctors and no other assessments were necessary before asking them to leave. Later, Lynn admitted to another patient in the hospital that no medical examination had been performed, though we didn't believe them. It seemed like another ploy, especially after Bonet had previously smuggled in a "Chinese Herb Doctor" for an unauthorized assessment.

Meanwhile, Colleen and I were driving over a bridge near Clearwater during a heavy rainstorm when our attorney, Bach, called. "The hearing has been cancelled," she said. Dr.

Nedd, the rehabilitation neurologist from the University of Miami, had been unable to complete his neurological assessment in time, and his testimony was crucial. Dr. Nedd was the only doctor both sides had agreed upon. Colleen had flown all the way to Sarasota just for the hearing, only for it to be postponed due to scheduling conflicts. Yet again, we were at the mercy of forces beyond our control—another example of the constant delays and frustrations we faced during that time.

October 29, 2003

Maureen and I spent the day at the hospital, awaiting news on when Dr. Nedd would arrive. When Bonet strolled in, dressed in sweats, we knew Dr. Nedd wasn't coming that day. Bach later confirmed that he had not made it. She assured us she would go to court to present our case, including Colleen's travel expenses. By this point, we had become accustomed to these relentless delays and disruptions. Julie had now been in a coma for over a month. At 3 p.m., Dr. Stein submitted his assessment: "The EEG shows no change. The eye movement to the left suggests swelling on the brain's left side." He had reduced her seizure medication at the request of an infectious disease specialist and planned to discontinue it altogether. However, they were unable to control her persistent fevers. It was possible the damage to her liver was causing them. Every step forward seemed to trigger a setback.

October 30, 2003

This was Maureen's birthday, but it was far from a happy occasion. Julie was unusually calm that day—a stark contrast to how she had been. Colleen was still in town, and wherever we went, she rode in the cramped rumble seat of the Mercedes. That evening, we took a walk, had a beer at a sidewalk café in St. Armands Circle, and observed the people around us. The sight of countless face-lifts and cosmetic surgeries was hard to ignore: Ms. Face Lift, Ms. Lipo Job, Ms. Boob Job. People-watching had never been so unsettling. As we walked back to Julie's house, we came across two birds in a fierce struggle on the front lawn. An owl had attacked a seagull, and as it looked at us, it flew away, gripping the seagull in its claws. It was a brutal scene, a raw display of nature at its most primal.

October 31, 2003

I was still trying to sort out the titles for Julie's Porsche and Mercedes. I decided to consult Atty. O'Day, hoping he could secure them when no one else had been able to. My thoughts kept returning to Dr. Nedd and the rescheduled neurological assessment. Perhaps this time, he would finally show up. Maureen and I could hardly wait.

Chapter Four

November 1, 2003

Dr. Kester Nedd was originally scheduled to conduct his neurological assessment on Julie today. However, after several appointments being scheduled, canceled, and rescheduled, we were skeptical that this one would even take place. To clear her mind, Maureen embarked on one of her vigorous power walks across the Ringling Bridge, something she often did to maintain both her fitness and sanity.

Later, Babette Bach, our guardianship attorney, called with an update. "The third assessment will take place at 10:30 this morning," she informed us.

We arrived at the hospital at around 9:45 a.m. A short while later, at 10:15 a.m., Julie's fiancé, Larry Bonet, arrived. He began doting over Julie, kissing her and speaking to her like she was a child, despite the nurses' clear instructions to wear gloves and avoid direct contact due to the risk of spreading MRSA, a highly contagious infection commonly contracted in cases like Julie's. His disregard for these precautions left both Maureen and me fuming, as we had repeatedly warned him about the dangers. Yet again, it felt like we were talking to a brick wall. Finally, Maureen asked Bonet to leave, wanting time alone with her daughter.

Dr. Nedd spent a significant amount of time reviewing Julie's medical records, with Nurse Mary Vasquez, Julie's case manager, providing assistance. Our nerves were on edge, not knowing what was coming next.

Bonet, unable to sit still, paced the hallway like a trapped animal. Colleen, who had tried to reason with him before, felt particularly uneasy in his presence.

The room soon filled up—Dr. Nedd, Dr. Davider Bhamber (Julie's primary physician), Nurse Vasquez, two other nurses, Bonet, Colleen, Maureen, and myself. The space felt cramped with tension.

Dr. Nedd began his examination by manually opening Julie's eyes and placing a tongue depressor in her mouth. He then retrieved a red and white striped towel from his bag, which was roughly 8 by 24 inches. A nurse held Julie's eyes open while Dr. Nedd waved the towel back and forth just inches from her face, repeating the action several times.

Julie, however, remained unresponsive.

Next, he placed a stethoscope on Julie's abdomen, drawing all eyes to him in anticipation. He then produced a blunt plastic syringe resembling a kitchen siphon, filled it with ice-cold water, and injected it into Julie's ear. While there was a minor reaction, it wasn't enough to awaken her. The cold shock should have jolted anyone capable of waking. It certainly had all of us wide-eyed.

The next step involved Dr. Nedd inserting a 6-inch-long Q-tip into Julie's nostril until it was no longer visible. Again, though she physically reacted, it didn't rouse her.

At this point, the scene felt like something straight out of a horror film. Bonet broke down in tears, while Colleen left the room repeatedly, clearly distressed. We were all emotional wrecks, even the nurses.

Dr. Nedd continued, scanning Julie's eyes with the towel once more, rolling her onto her side, clapping his hands, and even shouting her name. Still, nothing happened. He tried to get a response by squeezing her jaw, lifting and twisting her legs, and shining a light into her eyes. But the result was the same—no reaction.

After approximately 30 minutes, Dr. Nedd gathered us in an office for his report. He explained that he had used noxious stimuli, which no conscious person could tolerate.

In the midst of this, Maureen suddenly interrupted, glaring at Bonet and yelling across the room, "Don't you dare glare at me!" Dr. Nedd paused his report and chastised us, urging us to resolve our differences. Maureen, unfazed, snapped back, "This is about Julie, not our differences!"

Dr. Nedd then concluded his report, surprising us all with his optimism: "I am confident she will wake up," he stated. This was something we had never heard from any other doctor treating Julie. Though we remained doubtful, his words gave us a glimmer of hope. He did not predict her condition upon waking but expressed his intent to reassess her in 30 days. We had no choice but to wait.

Dr. Nedd's report was to be submitted to the court by Monday, which meant that Bonet and his lawyer, Robert A. "Bob" Jackson, were likely working on another legal maneuver. We anticipated they would attempt to use Dr. Nedd's report against us, but we intended to stand by the assessments of neurologists Daniel Stein and Kimberly A. Monnell, who had previously evaluated Julie.

November 2, 2003

Today was a quiet day, and Maureen and I spent it watching professional football, a rare moment of respite.

November 3, 2003

Maureen and I met with our attorney, Bach. Colleen was also giving her deposition that day, though Bonet was notably absent. His lawyer's partner, Edwin M. "Ed" Boyer, conducted the questioning, purposefully avoiding direct eye contact with Colleen, an obvious tactic to unsettle her. But Colleen remained composed.

The deposition was taken in case Colleen was unable to attend any future evidentiary hearings. After the deposition, we decided Colleen should return to Wisconsin for the time being. Both sides agreed not to pursue court action until the 60-day mark, allowing time for a medical and legal reassessment. That evening, I drove Colleen to the airport, and Maureen and I settled into a waiting game, unsure of how long it would last.

November 4, 2003

When we entered Julie's room today, we were met with a heartbreaking sight. She was experiencing severe posturing, with her knees drawn up to her chest and her hands tightly clenched. The staff tried to seat her in a chair, but it took until late afternoon for them to finally straighten her legs.

In the morning, Julie's eyes were wide open. For a moment, it seemed as though she recognized us, but her gaze soon drifted off. Those vacant eyes were unnerving, offering fleeting hope that quickly faded.

November 5, 2003

Another routine day, if one could call it that. Maureen and I had lunch at the hospital cafeteria, as we did most days. Maureen, though forcing herself to eat, was visibly losing weight. Until there was any change—either medically or legally—our days fell into the same draining pattern: mornings at the hospital, a quick lunch, a brief escape to the beach, and then back to the hospital. It was an endless loop of waiting.

Later that evening, a friend from Wisconsin called to inform me that a reporter from the Sarasota Herald-Tribune was preparing to cover Julie's story. Though Maureen and I had tried to avoid media attention, I knew that we couldn't prevent the coverage. Our best course of action was to cooperate, ensuring the story was told correctly, rather than letting Bonet or someone else provide a skewed version.

Maureen was livid. She had never been so angry, convinced that Bonet had instigated the media involvement. After a long conversation with our son-in-law, Jim, she eventually agreed to cooperate. That night, while I thought she was writing a bitter farewell to the world, she instead crafted a heartfelt statement for the press. It read:

"Our daughter, Julie L. Ayer Rubenzer, underwent cosmetic surgery on September 25 and has been in a coma ever since. Despite receiving the best medical care possible, she now exhibits severe posturing, with her hands clenched to her chin and her knees drawn up. Though her eyes occasionally open, she remains unresponsive. It breaks our hearts that Larry Bonet, her boyfriend of five months, believes we have not acted in Julie's best interests. We have followed all medical advice and love our daughter deeply. We miss her every day, and we hope for a miracle."

Afterward, I wondered what piece of Maureen would be left when this ordeal finally ended, whenever that might be.

Atty. Bach called later and informed me that court

proceedings were postponed. I told her that the other side had no idea how much patience and determination I had. She replied, "Good, because you'll need it."

November 6, 2003:

We consulted both Bach and Sharon O'Day, Julie's attorney, about our idea of involving the media, and they both agreed it was a sound approach. Bach arranged for an interview with the Sarasota Herald-Tribune for the following day, and we also decided to provide a public statement to the press.

November 7, 2003:

We met with a journalist and a photographer from the Sarasota Herald-Tribune. The reporter shared that the story would focus on Bonet and us, as he had contacted the paper, claiming he wanted guardianship to make medical and legal decisions on Julie's behalf. This confirmed our suspicions— Bonet was leveraging the media to achieve what he feared losing in court.

November 8, 2003:

Maureen and I visited the hospital in the morning before I headed to the YMCA. That afternoon, we watched the

Wisconsin Badgers face off against the Minnesota Golden Gophers. Over the course of our stay, we saw four Badgers or Green Bay Packers games. Later, upon returning to the hospital, Dr. Daniel Stein, one of the neurologists involved in Julie's case, informed us that there were no further updates regarding her condition and, consequently, no neurologist was assigned to her case anymore.

November 9, 2003:

Another day began with "Good Day, Tampa Bay" playing in the background. I went for a brief stroll around St. Armands Circle, a high-end shopping district on St. Armands Key. Meanwhile, Maureen went for a power walk. At the hospital, a nurse mentioned that two young women had tried to visit Julie, claiming they were on the approved visitors list. The nurse, aware of how limited the list was, denied them entry. They wanted to know if Larry's approval would grant them access. Thankfully, they didn't get through, though I couldn't help but wonder how many others might have succeeded. That afternoon, Maureen and I spent time at the beach, reading and walking. As I gazed at the sky, thoughts of eternity and space began to stir. How long is eternity? How far does space go? These questions seem unanswerable, as both appear infinite. Space telescopes can view millions of light years into the distance, but what if we could place one at the furthest point we know? It would still be endless. Time, too, seems without beginning or end— even if the world were to end, time would not cease. It made me realize that both time and space are boundless.

November 10, 2003:

Our son-in-law, Jim, sent us a heartfelt letter urging us to persevere. He confessed that the journey we were on was beyond anything he could have imagined. He expressed admiration for our strength in the face of such adversity, emphasizing how proud Julie would be of us. Her spirit, he said, was guiding us through this ordeal, and though the situation was painful, he believed something good would eventually emerge from this nightmare. His letter was a touching reminder of the love and support we had.

November 11, 2003:

During our visit to the hospital, a nurse handed Maureen a letter from one of Julie's friends, Sherrie Holley. In her note, Sherrie expressed her deep sorrow over Julie's situation. Though still in shock and anger, she shared how special Julie had been in her life, and she fondly recalled how much Julie had spoken of us. Later that evening, during a phone call, Sherrie told Maureen that Julie's ex-husband, Robert "Bob" Rubenzer, had hinted at Julie possibly returning to him. It was clear that Julie's love for us was profound, and she would have been heartbroken over the dilemma we faced.

November 12, 2003:

During our morning visit, Julie showed signs of movement—her head shifted, her eyes were wide open, and she pulled her knees up to her chin. It was a moment that captivated the attention of the nurses, who speculated that Julie might be trying to wake up. Although she didn't regain consciousness, it was a hopeful sign. We also finally obtained Julie's jewelry, which had been appraised at $100,000—though we doubted it was worth quite that much. A nurse placed fresh flowers near Julie's bed, but when Bonet arrived, he wrongly assumed they were from us and demanded they be removed. Infuriated by his audacity, I later placed a single rose by her bedside, hoping it would provoke a reaction from him. Unfortunately, it didn't.

November 17, 2003:

We were informed by a nurse that Bonet had called the hospital, identifying himself as Julie's husband. Although the staff was aware that Julie wasn't married, it was clear Bonet was trying to manipulate the situation. I immediately contacted both attorneys, Bach and O'Day, and we started the process of gathering affidavits to file for a court order to restrict Bonet's visitation rights.

November 18, 2003:

Another shocking development. While speaking with Mary Vasquez at the hospital, the risk manager arrived and bluntly accused me of harassing the nursing staff, citing multiple phone calls I made to one of the nurses. Despite trying to explain the context, she refused to listen and stormed off. The hostility we felt from the hospital management was disheartening, especially after they had done nothing to stop Bonet's previous intrusions, including bringing in an alternative doctor to assess Julie's condition. It felt like we were fighting a losing battle on multiple fronts.

November 19, 2003:

The day began with Bonet's attorney deposing Dr. Bhamber. In a change from his previous statements, the doctor backed away from describing Julie's state as "persistent vegetative," simply calling it a "vegetative state" and expressing uncertainty about whether she was in pain. As we prepared for the upcoming evidentiary hearing, we met with Bach and O'Day to discuss strategy. We expected an aggressive counterattack from Bonet's side and suspected they might even try to escalate the matter to the governor's office if they lost.

November 20, 2003:

This marked our 57th day in Sarasota. We discovered that two of Julie's rings were missing, one being her engagement ring. While not ideal, we concluded the matter was closed after tracking down the missing pieces. Additionally, I followed up on a previous harassment call we had received, attempting to trace its origins, but the number was blocked. Later that evening, Bach informed us that Bonet's attorney had proposed a settlement. However, we were skeptical, as it seemed like yet another attempt to gain through a settlement what they couldn't achieve in court.

November 21, 2003:

Julie appeared to be in significant pain, prompting an

emergency request for painkillers from Dr. Bhamber. Meanwhile, the settlement offer from Bonet's side arrived, and, as expected, it was preposterous, demanding that we relinquish all the rights we were fighting for. Fortunately, our daughter Colleen, along with her family, surprised us by visiting, bringing a much-needed sense of joy and comfort after nearly two months apart.

November 22, 2003:

The pain medication prescribed by Dr. Bhamber provided Julie with some relief, and her condition seemed to improve slightly. That morning, I took Jim and the boys to a couple of pawnshops, where we picked up some CDs, including Merle Haggard and Johnny Cash. Later, we spent time on the beach before heading back to the hospital, where two of Julie's friends were shocked by the drastic change in her condition.

November 23, 2003

Maureen and I had breakfast with Colleen and her family today—our first outing since arriving in Sarasota. After our meal, we headed straight to the hospital. Julie seemed calm, which brought a sense of ease to us, despite how distressing it always was to witness her convulsions. Later, we spent a brief hour at the beach before returning to the hospital. Dr. Stein had marked "Persistent Vegetative State" in Julie's medical chart and bluntly stated that she would never recover. He also noted that, should Dr. Nedd return, he would likely reach the same conclusion.

November 25, 2003

We took Colleen and her family to the Mote Aquarium, and later, we met with our attorneys to discuss a settlement offer. We amended the offer, particularly regarding Bonet's visitation rights. It appeared the initial wording could prevent us from moving Julie out of Florida, so we added the phrase, "Wherever she may be." Our plan was already set to relocate her to Wisconsin as soon as possible.

November 26, 2003

Both parties convened at Bach's office to sign a revised stipulation and settlement agreement concerning Julie's guardianship (File No. 2003-GA14748 NC). After it was signed by all—Bach, O'Day, Atty. Mary Jackson (Bonet's attorney's wife), Bonet, Maureen, and myself—it was officially recorded on December 4, 2003, at the Sarasota

County Clerk of Court. The agreement included several key points:

All petitions filed by Larry Bonet, including the one under rule 5.900, were voluntarily withdrawn.

My petition for plenary guardianship would be submitted to the court without objection for my appointment as Julie's guardian.

Bonet retained full access to Julie's medical records and ongoing communication with her physicians, regardless of where she was placed. We agreed to respect each other's privacy when spending time with Julie.

I would ask Dr. Bhamber to clarify whether Julie remained in a persistent vegetative state.

I agreed to request that Dr. Kester Nedd's previous treatment recommendations continue, provided they were medically suitable.

Bonet could arrange for Dr. Nedd to reassess Julie's condition, with the evaluation completed by December 8, 2003. This assessment would determine Julie's likelihood of recovery and any additional treatments required, as well as whether she was capable of making her own medical decisions.

Bonet waived any previous objections to Julie's medical treatment decisions made between September 25, 2003, and the date of the agreement.

Bonet agreed not to object to the withholding of life-prolonging procedures if Dr. Nedd concluded that Julie had no reasonable chance of recovery.

Both parties agreed to take any steps necessary to implement the agreement.

The agreement could be signed in multiple counterparts, all of which would be considered original.

Faxed or electronic signatures would be treated as original.

The court would retain jurisdiction to enforce the terms of the settlement.

This agreement meant our family could avoid a lengthy evidentiary hearing or courtroom challenges. The only thing left was Dr. Nedd's final evaluation, which allowed us a small sense of relief. We agreed to give Bonet visitation rights and access to Julie's medical records, wherever she was located, but no decision-making authority over her care.

Afterward, Maureen and I went back to the beach. We spent time reading, walking, and listening to music, like David Allan Coe's "Talkin' to the Blues." Perhaps things were improving, legally speaking. I found myself reflecting deeply on mortality, as each week we watched death creep closer into Julie's hospital room. For the first time in my life, I was witnessing someone die. It brought to mind when Maureen and I watched her father pass away, connected to a heart monitor, though we weren't in the room at the time.

My thoughts then drifted to my own brushes with death—two particularly vivid memories from my childhood.

I was born on an old farm near Leadmine, Wisconsin, where we lived without electricity. Our power came from a windmill and an old one-cylinder engine. I was around five years old when my father left me holding the reins of a team of horses. In an attempt to mimic a seasoned farmer, I foolishly wrapped the reins around my neck. The horses, spooked by something, took off at a full sprint, dragging me along behind them. My brother managed to stop the horses at the gate, saving my life. I was bandaged up and life carried on, but that incident could have ended much worse.

Another near-death experience occurred when I was

fourteen. By then, we lived on a 320-acre farm and had upgraded to a tractor, although it was a dangerous one. Our old McCormick-Deering F-20 lacked modern safety features, and one day, while I was plowing a field, I lost control. The tractor hit something, sending the steering wheel spinning. I fell backward, landing on the drawbar, while the plow blades advanced toward me. The sharp coulter knives could have easily sliced me in half. Instead, I narrowly avoided serious injury, although I did end up with a head wound. Once again, I was bandaged up, and life continued.

I've had other moments in life where death seemed uncomfortably close. The first was during basic infantry training in the Army in 1955. We were constantly harassed by our instructors, many of whom were World War II and Korean War veterans. They filled our heads with terrifying stories about human wave attacks by the Chinese during the Korean War, and we were often told that our unit might be deployed to Formosa due to rising tensions with China. One night, the first sergeant announced that we would be shipped out immediately. None of us slept that night, gripped by fear. The next morning, he revealed that it had all been a drill—a form of psychological warfare, but one I never forgot.

Another close encounter with mortality occurred during my service at a Nike anti-aircraft missile site near Philadelphia in the late 1950s. With Cold War tensions running high, the threat of a Russian bomber attack was real. We were constantly on alert, ready to defend the city against a potential nuclear strike. One night, both air raid sirens went off, something that had never happened before. We scrambled to our battle stations, convinced that this was the real thing. The fear of death hung in the air until we learned it was another drill. Yet, the experience was harrowing, reminding me of the ever-present threat of nuclear warfare.

Finally, during college in 1960, I embarked on an adventurous trip riding freight trains from Chicago to Los Angeles. The thrill of the journey was coupled with the lurking dangers of train hopping. Though I had enough money to travel safely, the reckless nature of the endeavor put me in risky situations, yet another chapter in my life where death felt uncomfortably near.

On the first day of our journey, we hopped onto a Burlington freight train from Chicago, bound for Denver. However, a detective in Galesburg, Illinois, caught us and kicked us off, advising us to hitchhike. So, we did just that. A high school kid driving toward Kansas City picked us up, and by early evening, we arrived. We asked him to drop us off at the freight yard, hoping to get information about the next train out of Kansas City. Unfortunately, he drove directly into the heart of the yard with his headlights on, which immediately caught the attention of a police squad car. Within moments, we were outside the vehicle, and I found myself staring down the barrel of a cocked revolver, held by a tense but aggressive police officer standing alone. One wrong move, and we could have been shot. Luckily, after explaining ourselves, the officer let us go, and we headed off to find a hotel for the night.

My most recent brush with death occurred in 2000 while on the Mississippi River. Six couples, including myself, rented a luxurious houseboat for a three-day trip. On a sunny Sunday afternoon, we anchored near a popular shore where several people were relaxing. A group of college students noticed the slide on the back of our boat and asked if they could use it. We agreed, and they gleefully slid into the river, repeatedly swimming back and sliding in again. I decided to join them, despite not being a strong swimmer, though I could manage with a dog paddle. The students made it seem effortless, but the second I hit the water, the powerful current overtook me, preventing me from reaching the boat. Desperate, I aimed for the shore, but despite my frantic paddling, I couldn't make any progress. Exhaustion set in quickly, and the realization dawned: if I didn't reach the shore, I was going to drown. With no one able to reach me, and no lifejacket thrown, I continued struggling until, finally, two men waded into the water and pulled me out— barely three feet from shore.

Maureen and I felt helpless and trapped as we watched Julie, each day, inch closer to death, with no escape from the inevitable. We spent Thanksgiving on November 27, 2003, at Clyde and Fran Reed's home on Siesta Key, enjoying the Green Bay Packers game with Colleen and her family, before heading back to Julie's place for seafood.

November 28, 2003

A representative from a Sarasota nursing home came to assess Julie's condition to determine if she could be admitted. Scoring her a two on a scale of one to eight, with one being the most severe, they declined to accept her. While at the hospital, we learned that on Thanksgiving Day, Bonet had smuggled two friends from Illinois into Julie's room, directly violating hospital regulations. A sign clearly listed the approved visitors, but Bonet disregarded this entirely. We also made efforts to recover all of Julie's possessions—clothing, jewelry, and cars—finally receiving her clothes delivered in a van from Bonet's residence.

November 29, 2003

Day 66 of this ordeal, one of the housekeeping staff expressed shock when I informed her that Bonet, the older man who introduced himself as Julie's husband, was not, in fact, her spouse. This deceit was not surprising given Bonet's consistent pattern of dishonesty.

December 1, 2003

Maureen and I went to court to be granted permanent guardianship over Julie, a decision Bonet did not contest. Word quickly spread in the hospital and among our friends in Wisconsin that we were officially her guardians. With this, we set the wheels in motion to move Julie back to Wisconsin, where Dr. Timothy McAvoy had agreed to take her on as a patient, and a nearby nursing home was prepared for her arrival. Our friend and attorney, Keith Haberman, would take over guardianship once we returned to Wisconsin. I arranged for an air ambulance, which could be available on short notice, and I imagined the hospital staff must have been relieved that Julie's discharge was near, as her case had likely been an immense burden on them.

December 2, 2003, brought a meeting between us, Bonet, his attorney, and Bach regarding Dr. Nedd's upcoming assessment of Julie's condition. When we mentioned the possibility of relocating Julie to Wisconsin, Bonet was visibly stunned. Though he voiced no opposition in court, we suspected he and his lawyer had something up their sleeve. It left us wondering what they had planned.

On December 4, we petitioned the court for permission to move Julie out of state. Bonet didn't respond to the petition, and Judge Donnellan issued an order permitting her transfer to Brookfield, Wisconsin, for medical treatment. This decision, based on the necessity of her care and proximity to family, allowed us to proceed.

The following day, we visited a car dealership to arrange the sale of Julie's Mercedes. Upon walking into the showroom, I immediately noticed the cold stares from the staff—they clearly knew about our situation, likely from

Bonet, who had been spreading misinformation. Their judgment stung, especially since they were unaware of the full truth regarding Julie's condition.

December 6, 2003

Bonet raised no formal objection to the move, but we were growing anxious, expecting another legal hurdle. The day's Christmas festivities, with lights and decorations filling St. Armands Circle, felt joyless as we feared we might not make it home in time for the holidays.

December 7, 2003

That was another day that will live in Infamy. Maureen and I made all the arrangements to fly Julie and us to back home tomorrow, Monday, Dec. 8.

The air ambulance, two pilots and two nurses would be ready to go. Her medical records were ready. The nursing home and doctors were ready. We could finally relax.

We did not tell Bonet about our plan for tomorrow, and did not want to. I expected trouble from him.

Atty Bach called and requested that I call Bonet to let him know. I was advised legally to make that call. I expected trouble. We suspected that Jackson and he had a card up their sleeves, but what?

Sunday morning seemed serene to me. I went outside to call the Interested Person. Deputy Sherriff was on hospital security duty and by coincidence was there. He read about our case wanted an update. "How can a boyfriend do that to your family? I described it in detail. I was not in a hurry.

Then I made the call, he would call me back. We discussed police work, my phone rang. I told Bonet that we will fly Julie to Wisconsin tomorrow. A BOMB.

"You have been trying to kill her since the 2nd week here, and I am now gonna play handball." Screaming violently, on and on, wouldn't listen.

Next was a lifetime moment. I motioned

Iorio to come over, I held the phone 2 ft away from his ear so we could both hear Bonet threatening me. The deputy signaled me to hang up. I felt severely threatened by him, and to this day, 21 years later, he would have killed me. Except there was an armed deputy there.

Iorio questioned who was that, etc. When who should appear? The Interested Person, in person. "There he is walking in."

"We are not going to have a problem with you in this hospital today. I want your driver's license and your license plates. You will be under surveillance".

He escorted Bonet up the elevator to the 3rd floor nursing station. Wherever Bonet went, the sheriff by his side. I followed them up, Maureen was there. She had no idea what happened outside.

At that moment, Bach called and said "I just received a call from Bob Jackson. He is in such a rage that I hung up on him thrice. He threatened to see the judge this Sunday morning and get an Injunction to stop that flight.

She refused to go to the judge's house on Sunday morning. Jackson said, "Come tomorrow morning, I will call Johnny Byrd, Speaker of the House and the Gov. Jeb Bush's right hand man to force those parents to fly Julie from Wisconsin back to Florida."

So there was the card up the sleeves. Another Bomb. The Schiavo Card. They were gonna get legislative action. Just like Terri Schiavo's parents. They were gonna turn us into a Schiavo case.

We knew then and there that we had to secretly switch

tomorrow's flight to today, Sunday. If we don't switch, we will never get out of Florida. On that day, Dec. 7, we would drop the next Bomb.

Maureen was an emotional wreck. Bonet dropped his anchor in Julie's room, never came out. We didn't dare go in there.

We had a secret conference with the supervising nurse. "Can you help us shift tomorrow's flight to today?"

Several requirements had to be met, or we would be a legislative Florida vulture victim. Phone calls, secrecy, fear of a hospital leaker. First time Maureen's right hand shaking, leading to Parkinsons 16 years in the future.

All the cards had to be in order, Inc 2 pilots and 2 nurses on short order on a Sunday. The Wis doctor called telling that the nursing home cannot take Julie today. They are set for tomorrow, not Sunday. I said, "Doctor, I don't give a damn if you get a room at the Holiday Inn. We must have a room today!! No ifs, no ands, or buts!!

Babette said it is our option about telling Bob Jackson about the switch. "We won't tell him or anybody else. He has been harassing us for 10 weeks."

The Sup nurse told Bonet to step out to the hall while they gathered what had to go. Bonet had no idea where we were going, and would leave the Florida players behind.

All down the elevator, she on a Gurnee, and loaded into the ambulance. Bonet was ordered not to follow the ambulance or be arrested.

We followed via a friend, the direct route. To the Bradenton airport was an indirect zig zag. We didn't know why. Yet. Everything was a rush, thru the gate, onto the plane. Rush!!

We took our seats in an overloaded plane.

They fired the two engines, taxied to the runway, and put the pedal to the metal.

WE WERE IN THE AIR, finally escaping the religion-controlled Florida politicians. We flew away from them in a 600 mph Lear jet.

We, on December 7. 2003, pulled the Rug out from under them, and escaped being forced into a 2nd Terri Schiavo case.

Chapter Five

December 7, 2003

In-flight, Julie's body spasmed uncontrollably due to the confining harness. We granted the nurse's request to administer morphine. Observing her in a sedated state was less distressing than witnessing her persistent seizures. My thoughts mainly centered around the relief of returning home after my harrowing weeks in Sarasota, Florida.

Two hours into the flight, the pilot started circling the airport for landing. Through the left-side window, we saw the runway, signaling our imminent landing. The pilot unexpectedly increased the throttle for another loop just before our anticipated landing. The Learjet's speed was approximately 200 mph at landing. The Waukesha County Airport, located in a city of 80,000 residents, operates as a small municipal hub devoid of jumbo jets and intensive security checks. Approaching the hangar, we were greeted by a teary-eyed welcome from about 15 close friends holding a large "Welcome Home" sign.

An ambulance awaited us upon landing. The emergency medical team swiftly transferred Julie off the plane to a stretcher as Maureen and I descended the steps. The crisp night air, significantly cooler than Florida by at least 30 degrees, was thrilling. I'd never breathed such refreshing air before. Wisconsin winters no longer elicit complaints from us. In Florida, it's as cold as in Wisconsin for me now.

As we arrived, Wade and Colleen welcomed us with warmth while the EMTs transported Julie to Waukesha Memorial Hospital in the ambulance. We encountered our reception committee, who stood behind the Welcome Home sign. A friend traveled over 100 miles from Chicago to attend. Everyone wanted to know about our dramatic escape, so I recounted it. Our friend, who had been informed of Bonet's earlier threat, alerted the Waukesha County Sheriff's office about the possibility of him following us in an airplane. It was fortunate that he hadn't acted.

Upon our return to Wisconsin with Julie, John Hillery, a close family friend, looked back on the experience.

On Monday, December 8, I learned that Don and Maureen intended to bring Julie back to Wisconsin. Let's make a 'Welcome Home' banner for the airport right away. I went to the print shop to purchase a big print. My friend called on Sunday morning reporting that Julie would be flying in by air ambulance that evening, arriving at 7 p.m. Returning to the print shop due to a last-minute schedule adjustment, I requested the banner be completed by 6 p.m.

A quiet, gray day characterized Wisconsin on Sunday. I waited at the airport alone starting around 6:30 p.m. with the banner until more friends and family arrived. In the deserted terminal, the only signs of life were a sheriff's car outside and an ambulance parked nearby. The sheriff's reason for being present was unclear to me as well. The plane taxied in, building excitement. Despite holding the 'Welcome Home' banner, we couldn't see through the cabin windows. The ambulance crew left after transferring Julie, and then Don and Maureen arrived. Don expressed his relief to be home, while Maureen appeared drained by the experience.

After ten weeks, the harsh reality of her post-surgery condition was just as inescapable for them as it was for all who had witnessed her in the hospital bed in Florida. Keith Haberman and his wife, Sue, hadn't met Julie in Florida. In-person interactions were a different experience than our regular calls with her. Despite our efforts to prepare them, the sight of Julie in her vegetative state left them in shock. Ten weeks after her cosmetic surgery, the reality of her condition was overwhelming for them, just as it had been for everyone else who had seen her lying in that Florida hospital bed.

The drive home from the hospital was extraordinary. Upon returning from a 10-week military deployment, the community was unrecognizable. Upon entering the house, Wade and Colleen warmly welcomed us. In the midst of the chaos, the new hardwood floors were a detail I had forgotten. Stress can negatively impact various aspects of our lives. Among the outdoor Christmas decorations put up by Maureen's friends was a reminder of the support we received upon returning to Wisconsin.

December 8, 2003

Maureen and I were called by the hospital nursing station early the next morning. The nurse disclosed to us that Bonet inquired about Julie's admission and sought permission to divulge the information. Overwhelmed, we consented. Despite the 10-week hiatus from driving, Maureen remained hesitant. Friends from her teaching past visited later, wanting to hear extensively about Sarasota's experience. They disbelieved as we recounted our experiences.

December 9, 2003

As Maureen and I tried to readjust to life back home, we discovered that Bonet had contacted the Sarasota Herald-Tribune on Sunday, the day we made our escape, alerting them to the planned move that was supposed to take place on Monday. Once again, we were reassured that keeping our last-minute change in plans from Bonet and his attorney had been the right decision.

Reflecting on the house in St. Armands, I realized I should have changed the locks earlier. It wouldn't have surprised me if someone else had a key. My concerns were validated when one of Julie's friends, Nancy Birnbaum, arrived at the house with a locksmith, arranged by another friend, Angie Reed. While Reed ran an errand, a blonde socialite—likely part of the Sarasota "Rat Pack"—drove into the driveway, assuming no one was home. Approaching the house, she peered through the window, only to be startled when she saw Birnbaum looking right back at her. The intruder fled so quickly, she probably had to change her clothes afterward! Although Birnbaum wasn't able to catch her license plate, we promptly informed the police and requested they begin monitoring the property.

December 10, 2003

Our family doctor, Timothy "Tim" McAvoy, who was now also Julie's physician, had just returned from Hawaii and immediately took charge of the case. He ordered another neurological evaluation and confirmed that Julie's posturing was not due to the infections. He planned to transfer her to a nursing home as soon as we finalized her guardianship in Wisconsin. However, more harassment followed when the hospital nurse informed us that Bonet had called the previous night, insisting that Julie be transferred to another hospital. I reported the incident to our Sarasota attorney, Babette Bach, who suggested we get an affidavit from the nurse detailing the episode. If we could secure this statement in writing, it might be possible to have the settlement agreement rescinded by the judge.

The Sarasota Herald-Tribune later published a story on Julie's transfer to Wisconsin by air ambulance (See "Comatose Woman Flown to Wisconsin; Parents Flew Her via Air Ambulance" by Tom Bayles. You can find the article by searching "Julie Rubenzer" on their website and browsing through the list of articles in reverse chronological order).

December 11, 2003

Dr. Brian L. Chapman, a neurologist at Waukesha Memorial Hospital, became the third doctor to diagnose Julie as being in a persistent vegetative state. After this devastating confirmation, Maureen and I made the difficult decision to transfer Julie to Woodland Medical Center, aware this would likely be her final destination. The move was emotionally taxing for all of us, particularly for Colleen, who had lost her father-in-law at the same facility 18 months prior. I shared Bonet's request to transfer Julie to a different hospital with Dr. McAvoy, along with my failed attempts to obtain a written statement from the nurse who received the call. Dr. McAvoy acted swiftly, ordering the supervising nurse to draft the report, but she later informed us that the hospital's risk manager had blocked the request. It was an all too familiar response, eerily reminiscent of what we had experienced at Doctors Hospital in Sarasota.

December 20, 2003

Maureen spent countless hours with Julie at the nursing home, where stringent infection control protocols required everyone in the room to wear gloves and face masks. Despite Julie's declining health, Maureen remained convinced that

Julie could sense her presence. Her condition, however, continued to worsen, much like it had at Doctors Hospital. Around this time, we were informed by Atty. Bach that Bonet's lawyer had filed a complaint, alleging that Bonet was unable to get medical updates about Julie over the phone, as outlined in the settlement agreement. To prevent unauthorized access to Julie's room, we had implemented a four-digit security code—2222—of which Bonet was unaware. Frustrated, Bonet escalated the issue through his lawyer, but we ensured he received the code shortly thereafter.

December 23, 2003

Amid the overwhelming stress, Maureen somehow managed to decorate our home for Christmas. Before heading to Darlington to pick up my older brother, I visited Julie at Woodland Medical Center. Her condition had significantly worsened—her fever was spiking, pneumonia had taken hold, and her breathing had become labored and shallow. I left the hospital with a heavy heart, believing it would be the last time I'd see her alive.

December 24, 2003

Christmas Eve Julie's health deteriorated dramatically over the next 24 hours. Her fever climbed dangerously high, and her breathing became increasingly rapid and shallow. It was heartbreaking to witness how quickly she was declining.

December 25, 2003

Christmas Day At 3 a.m., we received a call from Woodland Medical Center. The nurse on the line informed us that Julie's blood oxygen levels were dropping and that death was imminent. "It could happen within hours, or perhaps days," she said. Our family rushed to the nursing home, knowing these might be Julie's final hours. Meanwhile, we learned that Bonet had called the facility multiple times, his only concern being whether the feeding tube remained attached. Julie was so severely contracted that she lay curled in a fetal position, her knees drawn to her chest, her fists clenched tight. It was impossible to imagine she could survive much longer. The nursing home staff began administering morphine, the only comfort they could offer her at that stage.

Maureen later penned an entry in her journal: "I sat beside Julie and told her she'd make a perfect Christmas angel. I assured her she had suffered enough and could let go. We knew this would be our final goodbye."

December 26, 2003

At 3:30 a.m., the phone rang again. Julie had passed away at around 3 a.m. As heart-wrenching as it was, we were grateful she passed naturally, sparing us from making difficult decisions about life support or engaging in further legal conflicts with Bonet. After receiving the news, Maureen and I stayed awake through the night before meeting with the funeral director in the morning. We decided to have Julie cremated, and her ashes placed in a niche at Prairie Home Cemetery, close to our home. I notified all involved parties in Florida, including the Sarasota Herald-Tribune, and asked Atty. Bach to inform Bonet's lawyer that, if Bonet attempted to attend the funeral, the police would be present. The funeral home was also notified of the arrangement.

We also discussed whether our wrongful death attorney, Rich Filson, would request an autopsy for evidence in a possible criminal case. This caught the funeral director's attention. We explained the details of the Florida situation, which left her shocked. She contacted the Waukesha County Medical Examiner's Office, and they indeed requested an autopsy. Wade, who hadn't seen Julie since September, was unable to bear seeing her body in its current state. I tried to comfort him by explaining that we had seen her look even worse during her 13-week ordeal. Despite the tragedy, her death brought a sense of relief—for her and for us. I remember Maureen speaking softly over her body, "Julie, we wanted you with us much longer than 38 years."

December 27, 2003

As we took down the Christmas decorations, we made funeral arrangements for Julie. Although creating memory boards from photo albums was painful, the cemetery visit proved to be the most challenging for me. Feeling overwhelmed, I wept while writing the check for Julie's final resting place. It signaled an emotional farewell.

While bidding farewell to another family, I observed the Ayers family outside, examining the Autumn Garden courtyard. I granted them autonomy in their investigation. Seeing them embrace revealed the depth of their sorrow. Don and Maureen presented themselves, mentioning their need for a location to rest their daughter's ashes. The intensity of their pain was obvious. We went outside to see the water feature where they had chosen to set up. Wade and

Colleen acknowledged Julie's affinity for the water, expressing that she would have enjoyed the location. Inside, overwhelmed by emotion, Don hesitated before writing the check for the niche. Among the toughest challenges he had faced was this one.

I later received a confirmation letter from the cemetery that the inscription on Julie's niche now reads: "Your happy smile, your lovely face, no one can fill your vacant place."

The Waukesha County Medical Examiner performed an autopsy on Julie, as reported by The Sarasota Herald-Tribune on December 29, 2003. An article with the title "She Could Just Command a Room: Unanswered Questions After a Woman's Death Following Cosmetic Surgery" was published in The Freeman in Waukesha by Sheila Ahern.

We themed Julie's funeral as "My Guardian Angel" on December 30, 2003. 10 to 11 a.m. was the time for the visitation, officiated by Rev. Norman Sylvester, who spoke under the theme "Life is Good," was a longtime family friend of Julie. Robert Rubenzer, Julie's former spouse and the girls' father, was present among the two hundred mourners with their two daughters. We were taken aback by the sizeable crowd. I and six others spoke during the service. Since many were inquiring about the Florida legal disputes, I couldn't help but acknowledge them despite Maureen's request. No matter the length or cost, we safeguarded our daughter's legacy against hijacking. Her life was extraordinary, and her death was unjust. I'll pursue justice for the unjust death that occurred.

Chapter Six

January 3, 2004

All Julie's Sarasota mail is forwarded to our home due to my role as her permanent guardian. One envelope among the usual bills we received stood out. A greeting card from Florida, postmarked on December 27, 2003 (the day after Julie's death), was found inside. The card bore a disquieting inscription. On Sept. 25, 2003, I know what transpired.

The contents of the card left Maureen and me profoundly affected. Initially, we believed it was an unwelcome prank or further harassment. We considered the possibility that the message was from a covert source linked to Dr. Dangl. The identity of the sender remained unclear. By what means can we determine?

January 4, 2004

I shared the card details with our attorneys in Sarasota. Each of them felt uneasy in unison with the others. A former prosecutor, Cynthia "Cindy" Barry, proposed the possibility of an employee of Dr. Dangl being the sender and recommended a handwriting analysis. A prosecutor might jump to that conclusion.

January 9, 2004

Colleen unexpectedly called us. The news she delivered was startling. This is unbelievable, she said. I have recently reviewed the informed consent form Julie signed at Dr. Dangl's office on February 20, 2002. In the 'Administration of Drugs/Anesthesia' section, Julie had written: 'No breathing device if comatose from anesthesia on 2-19-02 – Julie Rubenzer.'

The text left us speechless. We found an unsigned DNR order among Julie's documents. The handwritten note matched her earlier statements. During the eight weeks in court, I was unable to locate this significant document. The possible link between Dangl and Bonet might have led to its suppression. Our fury was palpable.

NBC Milwaukee contacted us for an on-camera interview shortly after our story broke. Given the national scope of malpractice issues in cosmetic surgery, we decided to address media inquiries jointly. Media coverage must be aired statewide or nationally, not just locally. Ignoring NBC's plea, we focused on our own plans. In retrospect, I regret not clarifying our position to the journalist despite having more urgent concerns then.

We then got a call from ABC in Milwaukee with an entirely new request. Robin Guess, an investigative reporter for ABC in Tampa, requested an on-camera interview about their ongoing investigation. We agreed since Sarasota was within Tampa's viewing area.

ABC dispatched Susan McDonald, Colleen Henry, their camera crew, Wade, and Attorney Haberman to our living room for filming. The initial 30-minute live, on-camera interview was among several planned. ABC intended to broadcast the segment in both Tampa and Milwaukee. The card from "Seek and ye shall find" held the greatest significance for us. We assumed both the interview and the card would be taken seriously and broadcasted in Tampa.

ABC aired the segment during Tampa's evening news on February 9 and in Milwaukee's news on February 10.

Another NBC reporter in Milwaukee contacted me prior to the February 10 broadcast. At that moment, I was unable to focus due to my real estate firm's office move. NBC's reporter expressed his anger towards our selection of ABC, dismissively referring to it as the "rinky-dink station across the street." She claimed the story belonged to NBC because they contacted us first. NBC, with a larger audience, urged me to change channels prior to ABC's segment. I was shocked to discover the ruthless nature of the media industry. Despite the media uproar, we stayed loyal to ABC. I stood firm.

February 18, 2004—Another Bombshell

ABC in Milwaukee reported an astonishing announcement from Susan McDonald. Robin Guess from ABC Tampa called me. The sender of the 'Seek and Ye Shall Find' card has identified themselves. After speaking with the Sarasota County Sheriff's Office, this person contacted ABC Tampa. Robin confirmed his legitimacy through an off-camera interview. She inquired whether he had sent the card, to which he responded affirmatively. She inquired about the card's message to confirm. "I know what happened on Sept. 25; you'll find it if you look."

The text left me in disbelief. A witness has come forward. This discovery could significantly advance the investigation.

Susan McDonald provided me with the man's name and

phone number. S.A.Y.S.F. (Seek and Ye Shall Find), who requested anonymity, consented to be interviewed on camera by ABC Tampa. I contacted S.A.Y.S.F., who disclosed that he had worked part-time for Dr. Kurt Dangl. He identified himself as a medical technologist, differing from a licensed practical nurse or surgical assistant in that he was not a registered nurse.

Dr. Dangl performed Julie's surgery without the assistance of an anesthesiologist or nurse anesthetist.

S.A.Y.S.F. remembered that Dr. Dangl delayed assistance for Julie, who had flatlined on the monitor. Despite the onset of panic and Julie's turning blue, Dangl refused to perform chest compressions. Michelle Lawrence was summoned to the room to check Julie's pulse. Though she considered herself a nurse, she lacked medical training and was unable to correctly take a pulse.

According to S.A.Y.S.F., after Julie finished coding, Dr. Dangl cursed at Amanda Fortner, the RN. Five minutes later, S.A.Y.S.F. started chest compressions with his permission. 911 was called as Julie resumed breathing. Dr. Dangl prevented the Sarasota County EMS team from entering the operating room upon their arrival.

I was speechlessly furious. While Julie lay lifeless on the table, I was certain that Dr. Dangl could have saved her had he acted instantaneously to revive her.

February 24, 2004

Maureen's spirits were flagging. Despite our efforts, Dr. Dangl's practice would persist, and Florida authorities would not intervene, as demonstrated in the Clara Scott case. Dr. Dangl had been the subject of a patient complaint from Scott, following an unsatisfactory facial cosmetic procedure. Although the investigation was ongoing, Dangl remained unpunished.

20/20's NYC representative phoned us, believing Florida would act on Dangl's medical license before the interview broadcast. Maureen's hope was renewed by this news. I hoped the media impact would compel Florida to modify its anesthesia laws as Dr Dangl knowingly and conscientiously operated at level III anesthesia.

March 3, 2004

An ABC Tampa reporter requested a response from us regarding S.A.Y.S.F. for an impending news segment.

March 5, 2004

A reporter from People magazine contacted me regarding a story. Agreeing would grant us national coverage and widespread reach, particularly in Florida.

March 8, 2004

The Milwaukee Journal Sentinel identified Bruce Crow as the S.A.Y.S.F. present during Julie's operation. Unbeknownst to Crow, publishing his name for the Milwaukee paper led the Associated Press to spread the news nationally. Upon learning that his name had been made public, he was taken by surprise.

We talked to Susan McDonald from ABC Milwaukee, along with Maureen. CBS was unable to secure an interview with us, while FOX failed to convince ABC to share their footage. The media buzz grew increasingly intense. 20/20 aired Crow's interview while keeping his identity hidden.

March 11, 2004

According to The Freeman in Waukesha, the Waukesha County Medical Examiner determined Julie's death to be accidental. (Refer to Figure 6-3.) We received Dr. Dangl's denial of liability from our lawyer, Richard Filson.

March 16, 2004

The medical examiner for Waukesha County, Lynda Briedrzycki, contacted us to report that she had finished Julie's autopsy. The cause of death was determined to be hypoxic encephalopathy and pneumonia as a result of complications from breast augmentation surgery, and it was ruled an accident. The cause of death was determined to be "hypoxic encephalopathy and pneumonia due to complications of breast augmentation surgery," with the manner of death being accidental.

Though reluctantly, I acknowledged that the unnatural death of Julie couldn't be determined as a homicide. This ruling could potentially protect Dr. Dangl from facing consequences.

March 26, 2004

Dr. Dangl was sued by Attorney Filson for wrongful death. Attorney Cindy Barry is arranging meetings with the state attorney to advocate for S.A.Y.S.F.'s statements on 20/20.

March 27, 2004

In 1992, we initiated the Trailbreaker Races, our

thirteenth annual charity event. This year, the event honored Julie by featuring her photo on the t-shirts. 941 runners attended despite the challenge of focusing on event organization. Channel 12 kept the memory of Julie alive through the community by interviewing us.

Colleen wrote Maureen and me a heartfelt letter about our family's tragedy.

Although late, this letter originates from sincere emotions and required reflection on recent events. Your bravery and fortitude during the initial three months filled me with immense pride in being your child. My most challenging memory involves defending our family's decisions for Julie in court. Your fighting ability leaves me in awe. Seeing Julie's actions, I realized the depth of a parent's love. I'm grateful for your help with her.

It wasn't easy for you both, being away from family and friends in a sad and hostile environment for three months. Despite the hardships, your love for each other endured. You held our family united, advocating for Julie.

Losing a child is a deeper grief than losing a sister. gazing at Justin and Ryan, I'm reminded of it daily. Our faith asserts that we'll reunite, happier than before. I hope you can find solace and strength in God during this time if you haven't done so already. The thought of our separation in heaven is unbearable to me.

I'd like to discuss my faith, which has been a source of strength for me recently, without coming off as preachy or overly spiritual. I'm grateful for your bravery. In an awful situation, your actions demonstrated integrity. I believe time, as we live our lives according to Julie's wishes, will initiate healing for our hearts. Despite believing we'll reunite as a family after death, I continue to agree with Julie that life is good.

With all my heart, I love you both.

The Sarasota Herald-Tribune reported that we filed a lawsuit in Florida, claiming Dr. Dangl had given or ordered an excessive and lethal dose of anesthesia during Julie's breast augmentation surgery. The lawsuit states that Julie was administered 250 mg of Demerol, 10 mg of Valium, 5 mg of Versed, 15 mg of ketamine, and received an IV drip of Propofol (diprivan). Following Julie's cardiac arrest, Dr. Dangl reportedly asked the paramedics to exit the operating room to allow him to complete the surgery. In a lawsuit, it was claimed that a fatal office surgery was due to medical negligence. Search the Sarasota Herald-Tribune site for the article about Julie Rubenzer.

Florida police were probing Julie's death for potential criminal charges, according to a later report by the Milwaukee Journal Sentinel. Police are now investigating the death of a woman following her plastic surgery.

March 31, 2004

During her doctor's visit, Maureen was relieved to learn that her blood pressure had dropped significantly by 30 points. Under the pressure we faced, I was astonished she didn't faint.

April 2, 2004

Bruce Crow's letter to Governor Bush for investigation assistance was answered with paperwork by a staff member. 20/20's crew was preparing to film in Sarasota, but Amanda Fortner, R.N., the second witness, rejected going public.

April 4, 2004

The Florida Department of Health issued an emergency order restricting Dr. Dangl, according to The Freeman in Waukesha. He was found to have committed gross malpractice in September by inadequately administering, monitoring, and recording anesthesia during Julie's surgery. He could only perform surgeries at hospitals with an on-site anesthesiologist. Despite not having hospital privileges or malpractice insurance, it turned out he was still in practice.

In her journal, Maureen recorded her feelings of frustration.

With mounting frustration and worry, I watched as others continued to enter the clinic. Given the doctor's behavior in Julie's case and others, the emergency restriction was insufficient.

April 7, 2004

Four months had passed since our departure from Florida. Despite the DOH's emergency restriction of Dr. Dangl's license, Maureen was still convinced that no action would be taken on Julie's case. Check the Florida DOH website for information on the order of emergency restriction of a license.

April 8, 2004

The DOH limited Dr. Dangl to performing surgeries using only local or topical anesthesia, as reported by the

Sarasota Herald-Tribune. Margaret Ann Mille reports that the doctor was ruled guilty of gross malpractice.

April 10-11, 2004

Over Easter, Maureen and I made our first visit to our cabin, Northern Comfort, since Julie's passing. Wade and Romy announced their engagement. Our first joyful moment since the previous summer occurred then.

April 13, 2004

Humana, Julie's health insurer, announced their intention to sue Dr. Dangl for $432,000, the sum they had already paid in medical bills.

April 16, 2004

With friends, we viewed Lynn Sherr's 20/20 investigation into plastic surgery deaths. 10 million people were anticipated to tune in to the show following ABC's nationwide promotion. Friends and a former neighbor from East Lansing where Julie was born called afterwards.

April 23, 2004

We requested clarification and reminded Governor Bush of Florida's offer to intervene in Julie's case after not taking action following our prior complaint against Dr. Dangl. We inquired about the licensing and insurance prerequisites for cosmetic surgery clinics in Florida. The letter was disseminated to news outlets, Attorney General Charlie Crist, and the Sarasota County Sheriff.

April 30, 2004

The Sarasota Herald-Tribune reported that a gag order motion was filed by Dr. Dangl's attorney to prevent discussion of the wrongful death lawsuit. Although uncertain of success, the attorney's motion was meant to demonstrate his diligent advocacy for his client.

The hospital chaplain, Lionel Nelson, has placed a lamp and plaque, purchased from the memorial money of Julie's funeral, in the hospital chapel.

May 9, 2004—Mother's Day

Though emotions were settling down, Mother's Day remained challenging. At the cemetery, I was more affected than Maureen. The text evoked a flood of memories and tears.

May 10, 2004

Ever since the 20/20 segment, an eerie calm had

descended. Governor Bush did not respond to Maureen's letter regarding the restriction on Dr. Dangl's practice. Frustrated by the lack of progress in Chicago, Wade contacted the investigator handling Julie's case. The investigator informed callers that Dr. Dangl hadn't breached any Florida laws.

We have the right as a family to examine the statutes for any violations committed by Dr. Dangl.

We believed the case would be dropped at that juncture. A different investigator was now handling the case, according to Wade's later report. He obtained the captain's name, contact details, and that of the district attorney. We were told that Michelle Purdy Lawrence and an assistant were about to be arrested, with the necessary paperwork being prepared.

In speaking with Bach, she revealed that Michelle would cooperate and testify against Dr. Dangl upon arrest to save herself. The case would certainly explode if that occurred. Emotions swung wildly between sorrow and rage, one day uplifted, the next plunged. Here's hoping it doesn't last forever.

We found Dr. Dangl pinned between three investigations: the Florida DOH licensing probe, the Sarasota County Sheriff's criminal charges investigation, and our wrongful death lawsuit. We could only wait to see if any of them would release him.

May 14, 2004

The Florida Board of Medicine responded, but didn't explain why they didn't act on the Clara Scott case. The recurring thought in my mind was that if we didn't act, the situation would repeat itself.

If a doctor practicing without insurance is hit with a judgment, they will have their license suspended by the Florida DOH unless they pay the full amount plus interest. The doctor was required to pay a bankruptcy-dischargeable first installment of $100,000 to retain their medical license. Determine which version is accurate.

May 25, 2004

Dangl sought to silence the press, including me, with a motion. The Sarasota Herald-Tribune reported that Judge Becky Titus declined to issue a gag order in our lawsuit. The Herald-Tribune published an article about the civil suit over

Dangl surgeries without a gag order. Find Julie Rubenzer's details by searching for her name online. Search "Julie Rubenzer" to find it.)

May 26, 2004

The Florida DOH requested the state Board of Medicine to penalize Dr. Dangl over his breast implant surgery treatment of Julie. The Herald-Tribune reports that the state is seeking a penalty against a Sarasota doctor.

July 30, 2004

Dr. Dangl's attorney requested mediation to settle the dispute, which Attorney Filson informed us about. We deemed it acceptable due to it not being binding arbitration. We might consider their proposal before making a final decision. I waited for my monthly updates from the Florida DOH and Sarasota State Attorney's Office.

August 9, 2004

Florida took action at last. Dr. Dangl's assistant, Michelle Purdy Lawrence, was identified as a wanted person by the Sarasota Sheriff's Office, having been introduced as a nurse during our initial encounter. She wasn't a medical professional.

Guess discovered Lawrence's apartment empty with no sign of her, leaving uncertainty as to whether she was hiding from the media or had fled.

Dr. Dangl's office repeatedly hung up on the media, and the Sarasota Herald-Tribune contacted us in the afternoon for a statement regarding Lawrence's disappearance.

August 10, 2004

1:30 a.m. saw Wade's call from Canada (Winnipeg). Lawrence was in Sarasota County Jail after being arrested. The police reportedly warned that she would have a troubled night.

At 7 a.m., I encountered a brutal article in the Sarasota Herald-Tribune. The text noted that Lawrence lacked a nursing license. Unlicensed, she administered anesthesia and assisted in medical procedures.

Colleen notified us of Lawrence's arrest by sharing her mugshot online. The intensity of media coverage on the case was unrelenting.

August 11-12, 2004

According to the Sarasota Herald-Tribune, JoAnn Parks reached a settlement agreement in her lawsuit against Dr.

Dangl. Like Lawrence, she had believed him to be a registered nurse. An unlicensed worker participated significantly at the surgery clinic, as reported in an article on the Herald-Tribune website.

S.A.Y.S.F. called the next day, unaware that Lawrence was in custody. Wisconsin had earlier confirmed the results than Sarasota did. The Herald-Tribune reported that Lawrence had surrendered shortly afterwards.

As the story gained traction in Wisconsin, I was contacted by a reporter from the Freeman in Waukesha requesting to view my records. Colleen informed us S.A.Y.S.F. discovered Dr. Dangl's office was closed. I wouldn't trust it until I could verify it myself.

August 22, 2004

Maureen and I deliberated on the potential results of the mediation session initiated by Dr. Dangl's attorney, Kevin Crew. They threatened bankruptcy and demanded a confidentiality agreement while offering us money. We wouldn't sign a confidentiality agreement unless Julie's estate received a monetary settlement. Since Julie's will named her stepdaughters as beneficiaries, we wouldn't get any money from her estate.

These authorities failed to take action against Dr. Dangl's practice. Our lawsuit for wrongful death aimed to put the case before a jury and secure a verdict. Failing to pay for medical malpractice insurance would result in Dr. Dangl's license being suspended by the state. We'll distinguish reality from myth now.

August 26, 2004

I spoke with both Nurse Mary Vasquez and Lindell Orr, president of Doctors Hospital, in separate meetings. The hospital staff's world-class care was deeply appreciated by our family. Peers oversee doctors with hospital privileges, enabling a self-correcting system that identifies and rectifies mistakes. It wasn't until we experienced it ourselves that we became aware of the isolation faced by those without privileges.

I paid a brief visit to Dr. Bhamber's office. Dr. Bhamber regretted his involvement in Julie's case and believed leaving Sarasota on Sunday instead of Monday was a crucial decision.

I later encountered a past patient of Dr. Dangl's who

shared a negative experience at the Cosmetic Surgery Center. To protect her identity, we called her Anonymous Former Patient (A.F.P.). The woman decided to face the Sarasota State Attorney's office regarding Julie's case. I hoped for her success.

AFP narrated her account.

In July 1999, she went to see Dr. Dangl based on a friend's recommendation who had undergone a successful fat transfer. To add fullness to her thin face, she chose the same surgical procedure. Michelle Purdy, introducing herself as Dr. Dangl's nurse, displayed previous work samples for his consideration before approving her as an ideal candidate.

In July 1999, she underwent surgery on a Thursday. Her face was severely swollen, while the left thigh was almost completely black and extremely painful, with significant bruising on both thighs. Michelle and Dr. Dangl reassured her that the bruising was normal. Although Michelle pleaded for her return earlier due to her concern, Michelle instructed her to wait until Monday for a follow-up appointment.

By Monday, Dr. Dangl was deeply concerned about the deteriorating state of her thigh and face. Suspecting a severe infection, they rushed to administer treatment, including two IV drip bags. Dr. Dangl contacted several hospitals to find a hyperbaric machine, eventually securing treatment at Sarasota Memorial Hospital. An infectious disease doctor there confirmed that the skin on her leg was dying. Over the following months, she endured agonizing debridement procedures in Dr. Dangl's office, but her wound failed to heal correctly, resulting in a large scar resembling a burn.

A.F.P. had previously sued Dr. Dangl, but the case left her disappointed due to inadequate legal representation. She had moved past the ordeal until she heard about Julie's case in the news, which reignited her anger and frustration.

We always wondered who was pushing for hyperbaric treatment for Julie. Finding out that Dr. Dangl had recommended the same treatment for A.F.P. after her cosmetic surgery complications hinted at a possible connection between Dangl and Bonet.

November 2004

I arrived early for the mediation session. The meeting was held in the same room where Bonet's lawyer had previously deposed Dr. Bhamber the year before. I learned that mediation is a less formal process aimed at reaching a financial settlement to avoid going to trial, with each side presenting their arguments before separating for private negotiations.

Before we went in, Attorney Filson advised me to remain silent, which I was happy to do, as I had no intention of speaking. The mediator emphasized keeping emotions at bay, stating that monetary compensation was the sole remedy in civil cases. He expressed regret over what happened to Julie but reminded us that no amount of money could bring her back.

I sat between Filson and his co-counsel, Cynthia Barry, while Dr. Dangl and his lawyer, Kevin Crew, sat opposite us. After Filson laid out our case, Crew made his argument, saying that Dangl was deeply affected by Julie's death. Crew then asked me to listen to Dangl's situation for 15 minutes, so I set aside my legal pad and listened.

As Crew spoke, I found myself feeling sympathetic toward Dangl. I visualized the Scales of Justice, with Julie's life weighing heavily on one side and Dangl's circumstances on the other. While Dangl faced a challenging situation, he was still alive. Unlike his previously arrogant appearances on TV, he now seemed genuinely sorrowful and burdened. Even if his demeanor was coached by his lawyer, it felt sincere, and I began to pity him.

I pictured a battlefield, marred by tragedy—not just Julie's loss but also the impact on Dangl and those connected to him. The surgery on September 25, 2003, had left emotional scars that I had not previously considered.

Despite hours of mediation, no agreement was reached. Filson and I decided that we would either settle for a significant amount or nothing at all. For me, this was about more than just money—I wanted to hold Dangl accountable for his actions.

Later that evening, I went to a steakhouse in Sarasota with two of Julie's friends, Angie Reed and Nancy Birnbaum. While we were seated at a bar table, I noticed Attorney Crew talking to someone nearby. I called him over, and we exchanged a few words. I told him how moving his statement had been during mediation when he described Dangl's devastation. I admitted that, based on Dangl's previous media appearances, I had assumed he didn't care. I remarked that Crew's challenge was that he was on the wrong side of the case. I sensed Crew shared this sentiment, although he didn't explicitly say so. He praised my conduct during the mediation, and it became clear that the attorneys, including Dangl, had been concerned that I might lose my temper.

August 27, 2004

I was scheduled to fly back to Wisconsin on an early flight from Tampa. As I drove past Doctors Hospital at 3:30 a.m., I realized it would likely be my last time seeing it. In my rearview mirror, I again envisioned a battlefield. Though the conflict had quieted during the winter, it was clear that it had reignited, and now I was no longer on the defensive. The ongoing struggle would undoubtedly award more symbolic "purple hearts." I wondered if I'd be watching the events from afar, 1,400 miles away in Wisconsin.

September 14, 2004

As autumn approached, Maureen and I began organizing our final trip of the year to our summer home in northern Wisconsin.

Chapter Seven

September 15, 2004

The past few months had been unusually calm in our lives, but sorrow and anger had once again found their way into our home. With the anniversary of Julie's cosmetic surgery on September 25 approaching, these emotions were likely resurfacing.

It had been a month since I returned from Florida without any new updates. The state attorney was considering further investigation into Dr. Kurt Dangl. We were convinced that Julie's death was due to criminal negligence, and only a jury trial could decide his fate. If the state attorney decided to drop the charges, my family and I would be left to grapple with unending grief and anger.

September 16, 2004

A call from S.A.Y.S.F. left me questioning the integrity of the legal system. The lack of progress was becoming evident. Although the legal process was slow, I kept assuring others that it would eventually work. Yet, the feelings of anger and sadness remained constant.

We often had to clarify that Dr. Dangl was not a dentist but an oral surgeon with a medical degree. According to S.A.Y.S.F., the Sarasota State Attorney's Office planned to take depositions from Dr. Dangl, S.A.Y.S.F., two other former employees, and Michelle Lawrence. Lawrence was believed to have critical information that could reveal the truth about the connection between Dr. Dangl and Bonet.

September 20, 2004

Susanne O'Donnell, an assistant state attorney from Sarasota, called to inform me that the Lawrence file had been assigned to her for prosecution. We were convinced that there was a connection between Bonet and Dr. Dangl.

I had five pieces of evidence that supported our belief.

During Julie's hospital stay, the interactions between Dr. Dangl and Bonet indicated they knew each other well. Their frequent exchanges during that time suggested a longstanding relationship.

Bonet had tipped off Dr. Dangl about a news story in the Sarasota Herald-Tribune, indicating a level of communication that seemed unusual.

While reviewing Julie's medical records, Colleen found a waiver signed by Julie, authorizing Dr. Dangl not to attach a breathing device if she fell into a coma during surgery. Despite the legal battle with Bonet, we had never seen this document in Dangl's possession during our court proceedings.

In Julie's final days in Sarasota, Bonet repeatedly urged us to place her in a hyperbaric chamber—a recommendation that was not widely known and felt out of place.

The A.F.P. article about Dangl mentioned his recommendation for hyperbaric therapy, which hinted at a potential connection to Bonet. This further suggested an ongoing relationship between them.

I shared this information with both O'Donnell and the Sarasota County Sheriff's Office, but it would take time for the full truth to come to light.

September 24, 2004

Tomorrow marks one year since Julie fell into a coma at Dr. Dangl's office—a devastating event that we learned about through a heartbreaking phone call. While at Camp Northern Comfort, we tried to avoid reliving those painful memories.

September 25, 2004

Colleen informed us that the Florida Supreme Court had overturned Governor Bush's decision in the Schiavo case. The idea of state intervention during our legal battle with Bonet seemed appealing. We felt fortunate to have a clear understanding of Julie's wishes, supported by the written evidence Colleen found—the anesthesia waiver that confirmed her intentions.

September 27, 2004

One year ago today, Maureen and I woke up haunted by the memory of searching for Julie's purse and being accused by Bonet of "casing" his house. Bonet handed me Julie's Porsche without license plates, telling me to drive it with makeshift ones. The memories were almost too painful to bear.

October 7, 2004

The Sarasota State Attorney's Office provided new details. Dr. Dangl's secretary, who also performed nursing duties, gave a deposition that was unhelpful for Michelle Lawrence in her defense of Dangl. Rumors suggested Dangl was paying for her legal representation, and we felt she didn't grasp the seriousness of the situation.

October 11, 2004

S.A.Y.S.F. informed me that Dr. Dangl had testified before Filson. The lack of intimidation from Dangl allowed S.A.Y.S.F. and A.F.P. to continue pressing for an appointment with the Sarasota State Attorney. I kept pushing them to stay engaged.

October 14, 2004

Wade requested a meeting with Filson and Assistant State Attorney O'Donnell. There was growing concern among us that the State Attorney's Office might not pursue charges against Dr. Dangl. If we won a wrongful death claim, Dangl would be responsible for the initial $100,000 payment, and punitive damages could not be discharged through bankruptcy. The focus of our lawsuit was on securing punitive damages, even as the potential for criminal charges remained uncertain. We anticipated that the Florida Board of Medicine would suspend Dangl's license at the upcoming November hearing.

October 15, 2004

A year ago today, Bonet attempted to strip us of our guardianship rights in court. It was a shocking effort to undermine us, despite Julie not being a minor. For eight exhausting weeks, we faced relentless legal harassment—motions, delays, and canceled hearings.

October 19, 2004

Clara Scott, a former patient of Dr. Dangl, reported that she had initiated a malpractice lawsuit against him despite it being seemingly beyond the statute of limitations. Patrick Corbett, from Insight Film and Video in Vancouver, expressed interest in producing a documentary on plastic surgery and malpractice. To avoid competing, I delegated the inquiry to ABC, who had been closely monitoring our case.

October 23, 2004

In the Sarasota Herald-Tribune, I came across an Associated Press article about the Terri Schiavo case. Jeb Bush continued the legal battle, potentially up to the U.S. Supreme Court. This family's intervention experience during Julie's case resonated with me. The case reminded me of how our family had to deal with similar issues of intervention during Julie's case.

October 25, 2004

I phoned the attorney. Request a monthly update from Filson. He planned to file two motions—one to quash the anesthesiologist's affidavit and another for approval to sue for punitive damages—at the November 10 hearing.

Colleen discovered the Florida BOM had changed the evidentiary hearing from November 5 to January 5, 2005. Despite the delays, Maureen and I remained patient. If the state attorney couldn't act on the evidence against Dr. Dangl due to the current criminal statutes, then the statutes needed revision.

October 28, 2004

In Florida, a man driving a Cadillac startled everyone at a political gathering when he veered into the crowd. The police arrested him unharmed but without granting bail. I was surprised he was jailed with no injuries, whereas no one had been incarcerated a year after our daughter's death. The nurse, who appeared ready to accept the blame, was the sole person apprehended. Lawrence was free from restrictions, but Dr. Dangl could only perform cosmetic surgeries with an anesthesiist present. We recognized the existence of two separate justice systems—one for the average citizen and another for the affluent and powerful.

Upon arriving on the fourth floor of Waukesha Memorial Hospital, I was reminded of the familiar surroundings. For three nights following her surgery, Julie stayed in a room close to the nurses' station. I was glad to find no painful memories associated with my current visit, my first since December. While volunteering at the same hospital, Maureen delivered flowers on the fourth floor and felt the same emotional response.

October 29, 2004

On the Florida Department of Health's website, Colleen discovered details of the legal actions against Dr. Dangl in both our case and the Scott case. Although our files were an inch thick and Scott's were half that size, their readability was equally challenging.

November 3, 2004

We watched as Florida voters approved a referendum on CNN, suspending a doctor's license after three medical malpractice incidents. Lawmakers' attention had been drawn to the issue of mandatory versus advisory suspensions due to our case and others. The triumph was minor. 2005's January 5th saw our wait for the hearing in silence. The legal process unfolded like a glacier, with intermittent progress and lengthy periods of inactivity.

November 11, 2004

I consulted with an attorney. Filson will discuss the Florida law requiring doctors to surrender their license after three malpractice suits, with a cap on their legal fees. Filson was uncertain if this would impact Dr. Dangl.

We debated two proposed court motions: a motion to invalidate the anesthesiologist's affidavit for Dr. Dangl and a motion to permit punitive damages. The judge postponed the first motion hearing to January 5, concurrently scheduling it with the Florida DOH hearing against Dr. Dangl.

The State Attorney's Office was readying charges against Dr. Dangl for enabling Michelle Purdy's unlicensed medical practice. A felony conviction may result in losing his medical license. Filson believed Dangl would file for bankruptcy to impede our wrongful death lawsuit.

Since last Thanksgiving, much had transpired between Maureen and me. Simultaneously, Dangl's license was restricted by the Florida DOH, Lawrence was arrested, and the lawsuit continued. The State Attorney hadn't charged Dangl, despite apparent criminal negligence on his part. We intended to travel to Sarasota on January 5 for the Florida Board of Medicine's hearing to rescind Dangl's medical license.

December 11, 2004

I was instructed via email to read about instances in the Herald-Tribune where Dr. Dangl's surgical patients reportedly stopped breathing, paramedics weren't summoned, and the patients were resuscitated using oxygen masks. Bruce Crow, the person who leaked S.A.Y.S.F.'s deposition, was identified by the media. Alleviating Crow's fears, I assured him that he would be hailed as a hero upon the resolution of this situation.

During a Christmas party a week prior, someone had asked me if things were beginning to go my way. The question was perplexing, and I answered with uncertainty, "We don't know." Some legal actions still remain private. The Herald-Tribune article, which was the first good news we'd received, managed to change Maureen's pessimistic outlook.

December 17, 2004

Colleen and Wade, respectively, addressed letters to the Sarasota Herald-Tribune editor and State Attorney Earl Moreland, with carbon copies to the media. We closely watched the Florida DOAH website for Dangl's request to reschedule the January 5 hearing.

December 20, 2004

One of Wade's friends is writing to the U.S. government. The Attorney General serves in Washington, D.C.

December 21, 2004

Irving Levine, the Florida DOH attorney, contacted us to discuss the Dr. Dangl case. The January 5 hearing will go on as scheduled, enabling us to make our travel arrangements.

Dr. Dangl reported Julie's case to the Florida DOH following a procedure complication. This report, released in November 2003, initiated an investigation that took over a year to lead to a hearing. Though it had been a long, painful journey, the pieces of the puzzle were gradually falling into place.

December 24, 2004

Today is Christmas Eve, tomorrow is Christmas, on December 26, I will commemorate the anniversary of Julie's death. Yesterday was Monday, today is Tuesday, and tomorrow is Wednesday. Today is Tuesday, yesterday was Monday, and tomorrow is Wednesday." Reflecting on the past year, I thought, "Today is Christmas Eve, tomorrow is Christmas, and then comes December 26, the anniversary of Julie's death."

December 25, 2004

Last year, we went to Woodland Medical Center in the afternoon. Upon departing, it was evident that Julie would not survive the night.

December 26, 2004

One year ago, as I woke up, our family received the devastating news that Julie had died. At 3:30 a.m. last night, Maureen and I both received phone calls. Several callers expressed their concern and recalled the significance of the day. That date, September 25, 2003, held the greatest significance for us.

December 27, 2004

Levine contacted us to discuss the potential need for altering our travel schedule due to a possible postponement or rescheduling of the case. By Monday, he expected to have a clearer understanding of the remaining issues. Uncertainty didn't deter us from planning a trip to Florida. I warned him about the possibility of Dr. Dangl requesting a continuance. After experiencing eight weeks of legal harassment in Sarasota last year, I believe Levine anticipated our readiness for any delaying tactics.

The January 5 hearing's witness list on the Florida DOAH website consisted of just one name. The doctor supporting Dr. Dangl in court boasts an impressive resume, encompassing qualifications in both oral and cosmetic surgery. I expected his testimony to validate Dr. Dangl's anesthetic agent selection for Julie's surgery. It's intriguing to consider how he would justify Julie being unattended for five minutes.

My daughter, Julie, died because a doctor broke the law, and the system let him walk away without consequences. Dr. Kurt Dangl knowingly and deliberately operated on Julie under Level III anesthesia, which is a clear violation of Florida state medical law. This level of anesthesia is dangerous and requires extensive monitoring, yet he went ahead, putting Julie's life at risk. And when she died, they called it an accident. How can this be? How can a doctor's deliberate disregard for the law and for patient safety be brushed off as an accident? Something is deeply wrong in America when a person dies because of clear negligence, and the responsible party faces no prosecution.

What makes this even harder to swallow is that while Dr. Dangl skated free, Michelle Lawrence, who worked alongside him, wasn't so lucky. She was charged and convicted for administering anesthesia in other cases and falsely claiming to be a certified anesthesia nurse practitioner. A felon. And yet, when it came to Julie's case, Sarasota State Attorney Karen Fraivillig chose not to prosecute. How can that be? It's not just an oversight—it's a miscarriage of justice. My daughter's death is no accident, and it's an insult to call it one. The law applied to Michelle Lawrence, but for some reason, it didn't apply to Dr. Dangl, even though his actions directly led to Julie's death. This double standard is not just wrong; it's shameful.

And if that wasn't enough, I found out later that Pennsylvania allowed Dr. Dangl to keep practicing. With

Julie's death on his hands, he was granted a medical license in another state. How can a state look at a man with such a record and decide he's fit to treat patients? It's beyond comprehension. Allowing him to continue practicing medicine not only disrespects Julie's memory but also puts countless other patients at risk. Pennsylvania's decision to let him practice is not just a lapse in judgment—it's a betrayal of the trust that every patient places in the medical profession.

My family and I have spent countless hours reliving the nightmare of Julie's death, searching for answers, and hoping for accountability. We have watched as those responsible avoided the consequences of their actions. We have been through the motions of hearings, delays, and legal battles, only to find that the system that's supposed to protect us has failed at every turn. Julie deserved better. She deserved to be safe, to be protected by the laws that are supposed to ensure doctors do no harm. But instead, she became a victim of a system that looks the other way when those laws are broken.

This isn't just about Julie—it's about every patient who puts their trust in a doctor and every family that believes the system will protect their loved ones. Julie's death should have been a wake-up call, a moment to say that enough is enough. Instead, it's become a glaring example of how our legal and medical systems fail when they don't hold people accountable. I won't stop speaking out, not just for Julie, but for every person who deserves to be treated with dignity and care. My daughter's death wasn't an accident—it was a preventable tragedy, and it's time those responsible face the truth.

Chapter Eight

On January 1, 2005, Maureen and I spent New Year's Day taking down our Christmas decorations. As I did, I remembered my last trip leaving Sarasota in August 2004, thinking I'd never return, but I was wrong. On January 5, 2005, Maureen and I went to the Sarasota County Courthouse annex for an evidentiary hearing concerning the revocation of Dr. Kurt Dangl's medical license—Case No. 04-2708PL, brought by the Florida Department of Health. It was the first such hearing we'd ever attended. Back in 2003, during our ten-week stay in Sarasota, Julie's fiancé, Larry Bonet, often warned us about an impending evidentiary hearing. However, delays and continuances meant that it never occurred.

As we arrived, a tall man in a white shirt and tie approached and introduced himself as Irving Levine, the Florida DOH attorney. He recognized us from the media coverage and escorted us to the courtroom. On the way, we crossed paths with Dr. Dangl, to whom I greeted, "Good morning, Doctor," but he didn't reply. Perhaps, he or his legal team were surprised by our presence. Inside, Bonet was seated at the back. It was the first time we'd seen him since "the great escape." We exchanged glances before walking to the front. The only media personnel I recognized were Mike Saewitz of the Sarasota Herald-Tribune and Robin Guess from ABC Tampa. No other reporters seemed to know we were attending.

The courtroom setup was typical, with the judge's bench at the front and two attorney tables—Levine with two women on the left, presumably representing the state of Florida, and Dr. Dangl on the right with his attorney Sean Ellsworth and a co-counsel who didn't speak during the hearing. At 9 a.m., everyone was ready, but the judge, Hon. Susan B. Harrell, arrived 15 minutes late due to unfamiliarity with the city. As the session began, it became clear the second woman with Levine was an anesthesiologist testifying for the state. Clara Scott, another plaintiff against Dr. Dangl, joined us, staying at our side throughout.

During the hearing, Levine introduced his first witness, Amanda Fortner, a registered nurse involved in Julie's surgery. Her testimony revealed that while Dr. Dangl directed the anesthesia, he didn't keep accurate records of the exact dosage. She noted that Julie was given more than usual to keep her sedated. Fortner also described a tense moment during surgery when Dr. Dangl lashed out angrily. Despite defense attempts to discredit her, Fortner's testimony aligned with what we already knew, revealing no new information.

Levine's second witness, Bruce Crow, described his efforts to start chest compressions during the critical moment when Julie went without oxygen for five minutes. The defense questioned his qualifications and actions, but couldn't undermine his credibility. Crow's testimony added no surprises either, although he was clearly offended by the defense's line of questioning.

The third witness was Bonet, who testified that he had taken Julie to the surgery and returned to pick her up. When asked if he had a personal relationship with Dr. Dangl, Bonet surprisingly answered "No." We were skeptical of this, having heard that they socialized and played golf together. Regardless, Bonet appeared devastated by the entire ordeal, visibly affected by the outcome.

Dr. Joan Christie, a Professor of Anesthesiology, was Levine's fourth witness. She testified that Julie had been administered "a lot of drugs up front" and the focus of questioning shifted to the levels of anesthesia used. The details around levels two and three of anesthesia were key, though it wasn't clear to us why, until later.

Dr. Donato Viggiano, a plastic surgeon, concluded Levine's witnesses by supporting the claim that an overdose, particularly of Propofol, had caused Julie's respiratory arrest. The hearing adjourned early that day due to the absence of defense witnesses.

On January 6, the courtroom was packed with media after reports surfaced that Dr. Dangl might lose his license. Ellsworth called the defense's first witness, Dr. Charles Draper, a plastic surgeon, who claimed Julie hadn't been given a dangerous dose of drugs, nor had there been a delay in starting chest compressions. We found this testimony absurd, wondering how anyone could defend a delay in administering chest compressions.

Next, the defense called Dr. Donald Caton, an anesthesiologist, who presented a more detailed explanation of anesthesia's effects on patients. He stood by Dr. Dangl's actions, although his testimony clashed with that of the state's experts. Both sides agreed that Julie had received a large dose of Propofol, but the state considered it excessive, while the defense found it appropriate.

As the hearing ended, Maureen and I left the courthouse, sharing an elevator ride with Attorney Babette Bach. I asked Dr. Christie about the legal distinction between level two and level three anesthesia. She explained that there was already a law requiring an anesthesiologist for level three anesthesia. Therefore, if it could be proven that Dr. Dangl authorized level three, he would have violated state law, which would be an administrative, not criminal, matter. This meant that Dr. Dangl's main concern was the potential loss of his license rather than facing criminal charges.

It felt like there was a gap in the law, leaving doctors in such cases able to resume practice after a financial setback, with no criminal repercussions.

After listening to all the anesthesia testimonies, Maureen and I came to one clear conclusion—the overdose of Propofol was enough to convince us that Julie never felt what hit her. Her intense convulsions and movements in the 13 weeks following her coma certainly appeared to be signs of pain. However, neurologists assured us that what we witnessed were merely reflexes, not actual pain. Despite our doubts, we had to accept the medical opinions during Julie's time in the hospital. After leaving the elevator, Maureen and I headed toward the building's exit—two large glass doors. Beyond the doors, we saw a semicircle of TV cameras and microphones aimed at us. I had never experienced anything like it. We stood there, answering questions as long as the reporters kept asking. Eventually, we gave individual interviews to various TV stations. Afterward, we had lunch with Bach at a lovely downtown restaurant with tablecloths. Overall, we felt reassured by what we had seen and heard during the hearing. We were confident that the state of Florida would either revoke or suspend Dr. Dangl's medical license, which would effectively close his Cosmetic Surgery Center—essentially a doctor's office.

After the two-day hearing, Dr. Christie, who was the state's expert witness, summarized her observations with this statement: This is the story of two days in court— the Department of Health versus a doctor, with his medical license on the line. I was the expert witness for the State. The Florida Department of Health's Medical Quality Assurance division initiates complaints against doctors, and major cases are passed to the Prosecution Services Unit (PSU) for attorney review. When malpractice is involved, they investigate and forward the medical records to a doctor in the same field as the one being investigated. In this case, I was the expert reviewer, having already gone through the patient records and depositions from the nurse and scrub technician present during the surgery when the patient went into cardiac arrest. The case had already caught public attention, raising concerns all around. As an anesthesiologist, I specialize in keeping patients alive, free from pain, and with no memory of their surgery. I have been in academic medicine for two decades. The questions surrounding the cardiac arrest seemed to focus on the anesthetic, so I was asked to review her records for the state of Florida.

It is never simple to pinpoint exactly what went wrong in the operating room, which is a hectic, fast-paced environment. The patient first needs anesthesia, and in cases of stress or pain, the anesthesiologist will put the patient into a deep sleep. A breathing tube is inserted, a ventilator is turned on, and anesthetic gases are administered while vital signs like blood pressure, heart rate, and oxygen levels are monitored. An exhaled gas monitor is particularly important because it shows if the patient is breathing or has stopped. In

Julie's case, there was no exhaled gas monitor. Some surgeries can be done using local anesthesia, similar to the Novocain used by dentists. Additionally, newer, potent drugs can be given intravenously rather than through the ventilator, allowing patients to recover quickly for outpatient procedures. The danger with intravenous anesthetics, however, is that respiratory monitoring becomes more critical, as patients can easily slip into deep sedation. Even experienced anesthesiologists occasionally face sudden drops in a patient's breathing. The key is to intervene quickly, sometimes pausing drug administration and supporting the patient's breathing through a ventilator. These decisions happen in split seconds, with very little room for error. A patient can survive a few minutes without breathing, but beyond that, they may suffer a heart attack or brain damage due to lack of oxygen. I suspected that the arrest resulted from an overdose of anesthesia, leading to breathing issues.

I wrote a report for the Department of Health, and they called me to testify. Julie was a young, healthy woman with no major medical problems, and she should have emerged from the surgery without incident. The courtroom was full, and I noticed her parents, leaning in to catch every word, exchanging glances. I could only imagine how difficult it must have been for them to listen to each witness recount what had happened. This was their child, and they had no control over the situation anymore except to hear the facts unfold in court. The case was cloaked in medical ambiguity, with no clear answers. Why did this happen that day? The media had already covered the case extensively, and now the lawyers were preparing their questions. The doctor sat still, his hands folded in front of him. The Judge would decide whether to recommend a penalty or let it pass. Would I, a bespectacled professor, be convincing enough? The questioning came fast. I explained the risks and benefits of IV drugs and why they can be dangerous. Did Julie receive an overdose? We kept coming back to the drugs. How much had she been given? The records were unclear; no one had written down the dosage of the most important drug. The nurse couldn't remember what had been drawn up, and the numbers weren't documented. Was it fair to assume she had received too much, or was this an unusual reaction? Despite searching for answers in the medical reports, there was nothing conclusive. I stuck with my opinion—too much anesthesia.

The defense presented their expert, a respected physician known for his integrity. His testimony was challenging, but he too had no clear explanation for the arrest. I breathed a sigh of relief, hoping the Judge understood the complexity of the situation. After his testimony, we exchanged smiles. I would counter his arguments the next day, and then it would be up to the lawyers and the Judge. I wondered if we would meet at a future scientific conference and whether we would ever discuss this case again. Probably not. Had I made things too complicated? I questioned if my explanations were clear after 25 years as a teacher. The doctor remained silent, the lawyers nervous. I thought of Julie and made a vow to do my best.

During our time in Sarasota, Maureen and I learned that the Sarasota Rat Pack had disbanded. I called Bruce Crow to get his thoughts on the case. Crow hadn't seen or heard the other witnesses' testimonies, as witnesses were only present during their own appearances. He was upset, particularly because the defense attorney had ridiculed his lack of a college degree, painting him as the least educated person involved in the case. Crow said, "No one believed me about what was happening in that office until Robin Guess's first story. I had to speak up. Dr. Dangl still believes he did nothing wrong. Two weeks after Julie's incident, he had his girlfriend back in the OR. He hasn't learned a thing. It's hard to find closure when you learn what truly happened behind those doors. If it were my family, I'd want to know everything. Now it's time for the next step. I can't help but wonder if things would have turned out better if the EMS team had been able to do their job properly."

Judge Susan B. Harrell presided over the hearing regarding Dr. Dangl's medical license and would make a recommendation to the Florida Department of Health. On January 7, 2005, the *Sarasota Herald-Tribune* reported that two witnesses, Dr. Donald Caton and Dr. Charles Draper, had testified in defense of Dr. Dangl during the hearing.

Maureen and I spent the night in Sarasota. On January 8, 2005, we caught up with the news and drove to Ocala to stay with friends at The Villages for three nights. By January 11, *The Sarasota Herald-Tribune* reported that detectives from the Sarasota Sheriff's Office had searched Dr. Dangl's office, finding employment records for an unlicensed nurse, but Dr. Dangl himself was not found. On January 12, 2005, a reporter from *The Sarasota Herald-Tribune* called to inform us that Dr. Dangl had surrendered to the sheriff's office and was arrested for employing an unlicensed person to practice medicine, a felony. Later that day, FOX News in New York City reached out about a national story they were planning, and we agreed to participate, provided it shed light on the high death rate from plastic surgeries in Florida. Patrick Corbett, who had contacted us back in October 2004 about a documentary, also called to ask if we would return to Florida for interviews. Reluctant at first, as we had just left the state, we eventually agreed.

On January 13, 2005, as Maureen and I were driving back to Wisconsin, news of the hearing in Clara Scott's case emerged. The Sarasota Herald-Tribune reported the arrest of Dr. Dangl following a search of his office, where detectives sought evidence that his ex-girlfriend had administered anesthesia to three patients. I thought to myself, "Finally, there's criminal action against the doctor, not just his girlfriend."

While we were driving north of Birmingham, Alabama, I received a call from Bruce Crow asking if I'd been following the news. I replied that we were on the road and hadn't heard anything. Bruce then told me that before the hearing concluded, Dr. Dangl had signaled his lawyers and abruptly left the room, never to return. Not long after, two sheriff's detectives showed up in the courtroom, apparently looking for Dangl with an arrest warrant, though they wouldn't confirm it. Later, a reporter from the *Sarasota Herald-Tribune* contacted me to ask for a comment, which Maureen and I provided. That same day, a reporter from ABC Tampa also called, wanting to know our thoughts on the situation.

As we made our way through a snowstorm in central Illinois, driving cautiously at 35 mph, Robin Guess from ABC requested an interview via satellite. We had to decline due to the bad weather, but we pulled over on Interstate 39 to give the interview over the phone. As soon as we cleared the storm, ABC in Milwaukee called, requesting an on-camera interview to air that evening, which would be shared with ABC Tampa. We arrived at Channel 12 around 5 p.m. to fulfill that commitment.

On January 22, 2005, I received an email from an anonymous nurse (A.N.) who had been involved with Julie's case from the start. She expressed concerns about the Propofol (Diprivan) that Julie had been given during surgery, suggesting it was likely the cause of the most harm.

She also mentioned that the Demerol doses administered to Julie, particularly intravenously, were excessive and no longer recommended, especially in such a short time span.

By February 2, 2005, the Sarasota Herald-Tribune reported that Florida's Board of Medicine (BOM) was recommending the revocation of Dr. Dangl's medical license due to his actions during Julie's surgery. While discussing this development with a reporter, I expressed skepticism, predicting the Board might suspend his license for two years instead of revoking it. That same day, Corbett called to tell me about a study conducted by anesthesiologist Dr. Hector Vila at the H. Lee Moffitt Cancer Center. Dr. Vila had compared outcomes from nearly 140,000 surgical procedures between ambulatory care centers and doctors' offices, many of which involved cosmetic surgeries. The study revealed that the risk of complications or death was 12 times higher in office settings than in ambulatory centers. Key factors included the lack of peer review before surgeries and the fact that anesthesia in offices was often administered by nurses or technicians, not anesthesiologists. Dr. Vila emphasized that anesthesia, as taught by the Florida Academy of Cosmetic Surgery, was often a common denominator in fatal cases, including Julie's surgery.

By February 9, 2005, A.N. sent another email to explain that while many people thought Florida's medical care was subpar, it wasn't necessarily worse than in other states. She had worked in hospitals both large and small across Ohio and Florida and saw little difference, except that doctors further from large teaching hospitals sometimes fell behind on current medical practices. She believed that the healthcare system was flawed everywhere, and it would take outsiders like us to instigate change, as it wouldn't likely come from within.

On February 11, 2005, I had my first conversation with Dr. Vila. His impressive credentials, including his position as an Assistant Professor of Anesthesiology at the University of South Florida, reassured me that he was dedicated to the cause.

By February 13, Maureen and I continued to closely follow the Schiavo case, in which Terri Schiavo's parents were fighting to keep her on life support, despite her husband's efforts to end treatment. We speculated about the motivations behind the parents' legal battle and who might be funding their efforts. Maureen predicted that Florida's legislature and Gov. Jeb Bush would try to intervene again, while I doubted the governor would reenter the conflict. I also suspected that once the parents exhausted their legal options, they might take drastic action to draw attention and gain martyr status in the Right to Life movement.

On February 22, the Schiavo case made headlines once again when her parents filed for an emergency stay with the U.S. Court of Appeals, which was set to expire on Tuesday. They also tried to have her husband removed as her guardian. The appeals court sent the case back to the circuit court, which issued a temporary stay until Friday, as the parents claimed to have found a new medical test. Their reliance on an outlier doctor, much like in our case with Julie's surgery, showed their rejection of mainstream medicine.

By February 23, a Pinellas County judge had extended the stay in the Schiavo case, and Florida's Department of Children and Families (DOCF) attempted to intervene. Maureen was right—Gov. Bush had reentered the fray. We watched the escalating public protests at the homes of Schiavo's husband and her nursing home from afar, comparing them to the quieter but equally intense legal battle we had faced. Seeing a Learjet take off near my real estate office that day brought back painful memories of our own ordeal, including our hurried flight home with Julie on December 7, 2003. Even the sight of luxury cars like Mercedes or BMWs triggered reminders of those harrowing weeks. At 10 a.m., in the middle of a business meeting, I received a call from a Tampa number.

I recalled vividly: any phone call has the power to change your entire day, and this one certainly did. I excused myself from the meeting and stepped out into the hallway. It was a call from Guess in Tampa, delivering major news. She told me, "The judge at the licensing hearing has submitted a 21-page recommendation to the Board of Medicine, advising the REVOCATION of DR. DANGL'S MEDICAL LICENSE. We need you and Maureen in Milwaukee for an interview via satellite. How quickly can you get there?" We confirmed we could make it to ABC's Milwaukee station by noon. The only new development was the judge's recommendation to revoke Dr. Dangl's license. The Sarasota Herald-Tribune reported that Judge Susan B. Harrell had found Dr. Dangl guilty of gross malpractice during Julie's surgery, recommending the revocation of his medical license. (Refer to the article, "Judge Recommends Revocation of Dr. Kurt Dangl's License" by Mike Saewitz on www.sarasotaheraldtribune.com, searching for "Julie Rubenzer" to find the article by date.)

Shortly after, Rich Filson, our wrongful death attorney, called to deliver the same news. Then, another call came from Irving Levine, the attorney who had handled the trial. All three were ecstatic about the outcome, but Levine's response was calm, which surprised me given he had won the case. Levine's composed reaction fit his personality—no dramatics. I congratulated him on his success, recognizing once again how a single phone call can transform everything. Maureen and I did the satellite interview from Milwaukee, while Robin Guess joined from Tampa. Afterward, we had lunch, went home, attended our grandson Justin's basketball game, had dinner with friends, and finally collapsed into bed. What a whirlwind of a day!

February 26, 2005 The Sarasota Herald-Tribune also reported the judge's decision to allow Terri Schiavo's feeding tube to be removed on March 18, stating he was no longer willing to approve delays in the protracted family dispute. The battle, which had been ongoing for nearly seven years and had reached every level of Florida's court system, had to end. (Refer to "Schiavo case gets 3 more weeks" by Mitch Stacy of the Associated Press, available at http://www.heraldtribune.com/article/20050226/NEWS/50 2260329)

This reminded me to reflect on things. One day while walking through the non-fiction section of a bookstore looking for a Pulitzer Prize-winning book for my collection, a question popped into my mind: How did Bonet find Bob Jackson when he was searching for an attorney? I doubted they moved in the same circles—after all, Robert A. "Bob" Jackson specialized in elder law. I realized that elder law covers many areas, including guardianship, and Bonet likely needed help with guardianship matters. Someone must have referred Attorney Jackson to him due to his expertise in this field.

March 1, 2005 News outlets reported that Terri Schiavo's parents had asked a judge to allow her to divorce her husband. We thought we'd heard it all by then. Bonet once asked me to sign papers so he could marry Julie while she was in a coma, and now Schiavo's parents were attempting to get her divorced while in the same condition. What could possibly be next? This was the eleventh motion filed in the case, with five others submitted the previous day. Reports indicated the judge had refused to hear the divorce request or any of the other five motions, giving the family until March 18, 2005, to persuade an appeals court.

March 3, 2005 Headlines revealed a Pinellas County judge had extended the stay in the Schiavo case, with the Florida Department of Children and Families (DCF) stepping in to join the legal battle over her life. A new intervener had entered the case, and Maureen had been right. Although Florida's governor had previously intervened, Governor Jeb Bush now utilized a state agency to get involved. Other headlines, such as "Error misled judge, Schiavo parents say," highlighted the judge's intention to review whether Florida DCF's files on the Schiavo case should remain sealed.

On October 21, 2003, we learned of an offer from a Florida Legislature member to intervene in our case, and I always wondered why it came from them rather than directly from the Governor's Office. Now, I understood—the special act granting intervention only lasted 15 days, requiring the legislature to renew it. It finally clicked why, on the day of

Julie's escape, Bonet's attorney threatened to contact the state legislature to force her return to Florida. The legislature would have had to pass another special law for Bonet!

March 9, 2005 During a case update, Assistant State Attorney Peter Lombardo informed me that no criminal statute could apply to Julie's death. Both Maureen and I were convinced Dr. Dangl's negligence had reached the level of criminal conduct. When I asked Lombardo if he'd like to see the statutes revised to allow prosecution in such cases, he responded affirmatively. I then took steps to reach out to Senator Lisa Carlton, asking her to consult our attorneys in Sarasota to see if there was a need to review the criminal laws. If she contacted them, I believed it could spark an initiative within the Florida Legislature to address this gap in the law.

Our message to Carlton explained that we believed Julie's death was an example of malpractice deserving criminal consequences. We also highlighted the efforts underway by the Florida Society of Anesthesiologists and Florida DOH to revise anesthesia regulations. We encouraged her to speak with the attorneys involved in our case and decide whether legislation was needed to address this issue.

March 11, 2005 More headlines emerged from Clearwater, including, "Pinellas County judge denies DCF request to investigate Schiavo case," and "Lawmakers prepare Terri's Law Part 2 as judge hears DCF arguments." March 13 brought more updates with the headline, "Michael Schiavo, brother, both break long silence in ongoing case," which reported a million-dollar offer for Michael Schiavo to relinquish guardianship.

As this case unfolded, I began to reflect on the right-to-life and right-to-die debates, realizing they could play a significant role in Florida's future elections. While it seemed like these issues would shape voter outcomes, I wasn't sure whether the public was truly paying attention.

By March 18, the media reported that the legislative push by Schiavo's parents had failed, with Florida lawmakers unable to secure a legal remedy to block the court's order. Efforts in Washington, D.C. also fell short, despite Republican leaders' attempts to pass a measure President George W. Bush had promised to sign. The case demonstrated Republican opposition and even saw Congressman Jim Sensenbrenner from my own Wisconsin district become involved, showing that no one was truly distant from this legal battle.

Throughout those 10 weeks, observing Florida's legislative actions surrounding the Schiavo case, I questioned my allegiance to the Republican Party. I had assumed it was just Florida Republicans meddling in personal matters, but when similar efforts surfaced in Washington D.C., it became clear that the Religious Right had heavily influenced the party. Reflecting on past Republican leaders, like Eisenhower, Nixon, Ford, and Reagan, I felt certain they wouldn't have involved themselves in such an issue.

I left the Republican Party with a promise to return when it found its way again. Until then, I am staying away. My decision was reinforced when I read that President Bush had flown back to Washington just to sign a bill related to the Schiavo case. I found myself hoping I would live long enough to see historians reflect on this dark chapter in American history. As my wife Maureen and I watched TV, memories of Sarasota from the fall of 2003 flooded back. We kept seeing coverage of the Schiavo case, witnessing the public's support and opposition as it unfolded on TV. Every day, it was the same: many refused to heed the advice of medical experts. There's a term professionals use for clients who disregard their guidance: "out of control clients." That's precisely what we were witnessing with Schiavo's parents, who were dissatisfied with what neurologists told them and kept searching for different opinions.

Headlines told the story: Judge George Greer had ruled to remove the feeding tube keeping Schiavo alive, despite opposition from congressional Republicans. I admired Judge Greer. He was a hero, steadfast in his defense of Terri's constitutional rights despite facing threats and vilification, even from his own Baptist Church. Greer could have retired gracefully in 2004 but chose to stay and defend his judicial decision. He watched as both the executive and legislative branches interfered in what should have been a judicial matter, refusing to let political pressure sway his commitment to justice.

As the Schiavo case progressed, the political divisions it exposed became clearer. A CBS poll showed that 70% of Americans disapproved of Congress getting involved in the case. Even core Republican groups were divided—54% of conservatives supported removing the feeding tube, and the split among Evangelical Protestants was almost even. Yet, despite the clear public disapproval, the Republican leadership pressed on, driven by emotional, religious, and political motivations.

Watching these events unfold, Maureen and I were reminded of our own ordeal in Florida in 2003. Every time we saw Terri Schiavo on the news, we were transported back to that time, seeing Julie in her hospital bed, fearing we could have ended up in a similar situation. It was a sobering reminder that this kind of tragedy could happen to anyone. Polls indicated that a large majority of Americans felt Congress had acted out of political self-interest rather than genuine concern.

As the situation escalated, we saw that even within the Republican Party, there were growing fractures. A backlash was beginning, as people realized that the intervention in the Schiavo case was an overreach by Congress and President Bush. The religious right, though vocal, did not represent the silent majority of Americans, who largely supported the courts and disapproved of the political interference.

By March 31, 2005, the Supreme Court had rejected the final appeal, and Terri Schiavo passed away at the age of 41. It was a tragedy for all involved, and I couldn't help but reflect on the personal toll it had taken on everyone. While I sympathized with the Schiavo family, I firmly believed that Congress and the President had made a grave mistake by intervening. This matter should have remained a private family issue, handled within the judicial system. The Schiavo case left a lasting impact, not only on those directly involved but on the broader American public, who had witnessed an unprecedented intrusion of politics into a deeply personal and legal matter.

Chapter Nine

April 1, 2005

Being April Fool's Day, I couldn't help but wonder if someone would play a prank on me. Maureen and I were preparing for another trip to Sarasota. Since January, we had been in touch with Patrick Corbett, a producer from a Canadian company in Vancouver, who wanted us to participate in a documentary about medical malpractice in cosmetic surgery across the country. While we were interested, we were hesitant about returning to Florida so soon after attending Dr. Dangl's license revocation hearing.

April 4, 2005

The Sarasota Herald-Tribune announced that the state of Florida had officially revoked Dr. Dangl's medical license. (For more information, search "Julie Rubenzer" on the Sarasota Herald-Tribune website and scroll through the results to find the article by Mitra Malek titled "Dangl's medical license revoked.")

April 12, 2005

Maureen and I flew from Milwaukee to Sarasota on Delta

Flight Dl1095, arriving in the afternoon. That evening, we reconnected with Fran and Clyde Reed, friends from Wisconsin who spent winters in Sarasota. We hadn't seen them since they drove us to the airport back in December 2003 when we hastily left. We updated them on the case, and then shared a seafood dinner.

April 13, 2005

Our day started with the familiar morning news greeting, "Good Day, Tampa Bay," which we had heard during our 2003 stay. Our first stop was the library to check emails, then we visited Doctors Hospital to see Chaplin Lionel Nelson and Julie's memorial plaque in the chapel. Seeing the plaque, which mirrored her niche in the Wisconsin cemetery but with the wrong year (2003 instead of 2004), stirred deep emotions. It displayed her last photograph, taken in August 2003, along with the words I had written: *"Your happy smile, your lovely face, No one can fill your vacant place."*

After signing the guest log and shedding many tears, we left the chapel. In the hospital lobby, we ran into Nelson, who had spent countless hours with us during our stay in 2003. I recalled telling him back then, "We need more than prayers; we need a miracle." Upon leaving, we bumped into Steve Schwenker, who had known Julie and had been hospitalized several times due to muscular dystrophy. We reminisced briefly before heading to verify whether Dr. Dangl's cosmetic surgery center was closed. Maureen looked through the window, confirming it was shut down, bringing us a bit of relief.

April 14, 2005

Once again, the morning news greeted us with "Good Day, Tampa Bay." We met with the camera crew from Vancouver at 10 a.m. and, after discussing the case, we headed to Lido Beach, where they wanted to film us. The beach brought back many memories of our time there during those long 10 weeks. Seeing a couple with their two young girls building sandcastles hit hard, and Maureen struggled emotionally. After filming, we went to the Ritz-Carlton, where the production company had set up a sound studio in a suite. We were interviewed separately on camera. Later that day, we met Angie Reed and Nancy Birnbaum, two of Julie's friends, for drinks and food at an outdoor café on Main Street.

April 15, 2005

After hearing "Good Day, Tampa Bay" again, Maureen and I met with Dr. Hector Vila, a Professor of Anesthesiology at the University of South Florida. Dr. Vila had extensive credentials, but what stood out was his focus on preventive measures in law to avoid tragedies like Julie's. He also informed us that the Florida Academy of Plastic Surgeons, which had certified Dr. Dangl, had gone out of business. The academy, responsible for recommending the dangerous combination of drugs that killed Julie, could not be sued due to legal protection. It was disheartening to know that "they got away with it," as the saying goes. Our meeting ended around 2:30 p.m.

April 16, 2005

We flew out of Sarasota on Delta Flight DL 948. As the plane climbed, I took one last look at the city and the landmarks we had come to know. Seeing the hospital where Julie's memorial stood brought a flood of emotions. As we left Sarasota, Maureen and I agreed never to return. The painful memories were too much, and we knew we could never vacation there again.

May 15, 2005

Maureen suggested we visit the cemetery to change the flowers on Julie's niche from winter to spring. While I didn't enjoy these visits, I went along. As we stood there, rage and sorrow boiled up inside me, and Maureen tearfully expressed that she never thought she'd have to do this. Neither did I. It was a painful reminder that I needed to continue to focus on Julie's case.

May 24, 2005

Everyone familiar with our situation kept asking the same two questions:

Why hadn't the Sarasota State Attorney's Office charged Dr. Dangl with criminal negligence?

How could this have happened? The State Attorney's Office explained that after numerous meetings and reviews, they concluded that criminal negligence could not be proven. We didn't accept this answer, and neither did our attorney. Wade likened the situation to a drunk driver who leaves someone to die—surely, that would be criminal. Yet, a doctor doing the same seemed to face no consequences.

Dr. Joan Christie, an expert witness at Dr. Dangl's hearing, explained that despite our advanced medical system, Julie fell through a loophole. Cosmetic surgeries performed in doctors' offices were unregulated at the time, allowing dangerous practices to persist. While hospitals and surgery centers have strict credentialing and accreditation processes, office surgeries operated with little oversight. Julie had fallen victim to this lack of regulation.

By 2000, the Florida Board of Medicine introduced some regulations for office surgeries, but many surgeons, including Dr. Dangl, opposed them. He even claimed office surgery was safe and accused hospitals of pushing for regulations to protect their business. Despite some reforms, cosmetic surgeons continued to perform risky procedures in unregulated environments, leading to deaths like Julie's.

September 4, 2005

The summer had been relatively quiet, though the case moved slowly. However, we learned from Dr. Vila about yet another cosmetic surgery-related death. It seemed that, despite everything, these preventable tragedies continued.

Chapter Ten

On September 5, 2005, Bruce Crow, a surgical technician present during Julie's cosmetic surgery, updated me on Michelle Lawrence's trial. Initially set for today, the trial was rescheduled for December 5, 2005, to take place in the same courtroom with the same judge as Dr. Kurt Dangl, the surgeon who operated on Julie. It seemed that Lawrence and Dr. Dangl would be tried simultaneously, raising suspicions. Shortly after, our attorney, Richard A. "Rich" Filson, informed me that he had successfully obtained court approval to sue Dr. Dangl for punitive damages, with Dr. Dangl having 20 days to respond. After this, we could proceed to a jury trial. I had signed the contract to initiate this lawsuit nearly two years ago in October 2003, but we still hadn't gone to trial, reinforcing how slow the legal process can be.

I then found an article by Bob LaMendola in the *Sun Sentinel*, dated January 17, 2004. The article reported that since May, five Florida residents had died after undergoing liposuction or other body reshaping surgeries, including two patients treated at the same surgical center in Ft. Lauderdale.

The Florida Center for Cosmetic Surgery, which heavily advertised to minorities and gay men, claimed to offer "safe, beautiful, long-lasting results." Despite Florida having some of the strictest patient safety standards, cosmetic surgery deaths were still occurring. Dr. Elisabeth Tucker of the Florida Board of Medicine voiced her concern, stating that she would ensure the Florida Department of Health investigated these deaths to find any common threads.

The article highlighted several tragic cases, including that of James K. McCormick, who died the day after facial surgery on his 51st birthday. Jacquelyn V. Roberts, a 45-year-old mother, passed away two days after a tummy tuck and liposuction. The Broward County Medical Examiner had not yet determined the cause of either death. The center's medical director, Dr. Jeffrey Hamm, and its Atlanta-based owner declined to comment due to patient confidentiality laws.

The *Sun Sentinel* had also confirmed that since January 1997, 36 deaths had occurred following office surgeries in Florida, mostly involving routine procedures like tummy tucks and liposuction. Dr. Yoav Barnavon, president of the Florida Society of Plastic Surgeons, noted that while most patients experienced successful results, complications like pulmonary embolism could be fatal, and doctors needed to ensure patients were aware of such risks.

State officials had imposed a three-month moratorium on office surgeries in 2000 after a cluster of deaths and introduced new safety standards, such as requiring accreditation for surgical offices and limiting the length of procedures. However, in 2002, five more patients died, prompting further review of these regulations.

The article described other cases, such as Claudine King, who died in 2003 from a pulmonary embolism after a tummy tuck and liposuction in Orlando. Another patient, Maria Borrego, died nine days after a similar procedure in Aventura, while Julie Rubenzer, from Sarasota, slipped into a coma during breast implant surgery and never regained consciousness.

In December 2005, the *Sarasota Herald-Tribune* reported that Dr. Dangl pleaded no contest to a criminal charge related to Julie's death. While Maureen and I had hoped for a negligent homicide charge, Dr. Dangl received 12 months of probation. The paper also covered public outrage over the sentencing, contrasting it with a construction worker's seven-and-a-half-year prison sentence for a death caused by inattentive driving.

On December 27, 2005, *The Wall Street Journal* published an article about making colonoscopies more comfortable, emphasizing that insurance companies were reluctant to cover anesthesiologists administering Propofol. This caught my attention, as Julie's death had involved an overdose of Propofol during her surgery. I wrote a letter to the editor stressing the importance of having highly trained professionals, like anesthesiologists, handle Propofol, arguing that patient safety should take precedence over cost-cutting measures.

Chapter Eleven

On January 27, 2006, we received a copy of an arrest warrant issued in the State of Florida against Michele L. Lawrence, also known as Michelle Purdy (SSO Case No. 06-7437). The warrant, circulated to all deputies and police officers in Sarasota County, accused Lawrence of violating Florida State Statute (F.S.S.) 893.13(7)(a) 9, for "Obtaining a Controlled Substance by Fraud" (one count) and F.S.S. 831.30 for "Fraud in Obtaining Medical Drugs" (one count), with bond amounts set accordingly.

In August 2006, I received a call from a producer of Nancy Grace regarding a case where an unlicensed Brazilian doctor had performed liposuction in a Massachusetts condo basement, resulting in the patient's death. I appeared on the show but was cut short due to breaking news about Mel Gibson. Had the interview continued, I intended to raise concerns about the State Attorney's Office in Sarasota and Florida's lax criminal laws.

On August 14, 2006, the Sarasota Herald-Tribune published a statement from Maureen and me advocating for the Florida Board of Nursing to strengthen anesthesia regulations in doctor's offices to match hospital standards, requiring physician supervision and qualified nurses ("Board must strengthen sedation rule").

By September 11, 2006, I discovered that Bob Jackson, Larry Bonet's attorney, had moved to Austin, Texas, for new opportunities. The following day, Wade and Romy welcomed a 9 lb. 11 oz. baby boy, a joyous event for us all. Maureen and I visited them at St. Mary's Hospital in Milwaukee, marking our first time in a hospital since Julie's passing. The experience of holding a newborn brought mixed emotions, evoking memories of life and death, yet none of us mentioned Sarasota.

On September 28, 2006, Lorrie, an assistant in Attorney Sharon O'Day's office, shared an email summary with an anonymous attorney regarding Julie Rubenzer's case. The email detailed Julie's breast implant surgery, performed by Dr. Kurt Dangl, during which an unlicensed nurse, Michelle Lawrence, administered excessive anesthesia. Julie became comatose and was eventually transported to Wisconsin, where she died on December 26. Despite efforts from Julie's family, including Mr. Ayer, to pursue criminal charges against Dangl, none had been filed.

On September 30, 2006, I responded to Lorrie, praising her summary, and on October 1, 2006, the anonymous attorney replied with condolences, expressing sympathy for the legal ordeal we had endured. The attorney remarked on Florida's unusual legal landscape and explained their preference for practicing in federal rather than state courts.

October 6, 2006, marked the third anniversary of the day Maureen and I informed Julie about our decision to withhold life support. This painful memory surpassed even the day of her death, December 26, 2003. Over coffee, I mentioned that Michelle Lawrence would soon face the judge for violating her probation. Maureen, disillusioned with Florida's legal system, believed Lawrence would face minimal consequences, just as she had for practicing medicine without a license.

On October 9, 2006, Lawrence's court hearing was unexpectedly postponed, with a new sentencing date set for November 3, 2006. I wondered what might have caused the delay.

The next day, October 10, 2006, Dr. Hector Vila invited Maureen and me to speak at the American Society of Anesthesiologists (ASA) Convention in Chicago on October

14, 2006, where Julie's case would be discussed as a catalyst for change in Florida. We attended the event and left feeling more hopeful after hearing ASA's official stance that deep sedation should be administered only by anesthesiologists. However, concerns remained about whether states like Florida would enact stronger safety laws.

On October 17, 2006, I emailed the anonymous attorney with an update: Michelle Lawrence had cooperated with the State Attorney's Office, but her testimony wasn't enough to push criminal negligence charges against Dr. Dangl. Dangl had offered to plead guilty to employing an unlicensed nurse and accept probation, promising not to practice medicine again. Despite this, we maintained that he was guilty of criminal negligence. The anonymous attorney advised me to pressure the State Attorney's Office to bring the case before a grand jury, where the Fifth Amendment might not fully protect Dangl, potentially leading to an indictment.

Dangl can also be summoned before the grand jury (GJ), though he may invoke his Fifth Amendment rights more effectively since he is a primary target. Any witness called before the GJ is generally expected to plead the Fifth. However, they can first provide a "proffer" through their attorney, outlining what they would say. If the information is deemed valuable, the person may be granted immunity; otherwise, it can't be used against them. If Dangl refuses to cooperate after this is discussed verbally, you can draft the statement, and I can help edit it before sending it to the State Attorney (SA) via certified mail and sharing it with the media.

On October 18, 2006, I emailed A.A. to update them about my discussion with the SA's office. They were ready to accept Michelle's plea and were deliberating on Dangl's plea, with decisions expected that week. I conveyed our stance on Dangl's case, expressing that we believe he is guilty of at least criminal negligence for leaving Julie without intervention for five minutes during surgery and refusing CPR. This act itself constitutes a crime. Even if Dangl remains silent, two witnesses in the room have already confirmed these events. I told A.A. that Maureen and I planned to formally request the case be presented to the GJ, which the SA in Sarasota seemed open to, pending discussions with his supervisor.

On October 24, 2006, I updated A.A. via email (also copied to Bach and O'Day) that I had verbally informed the

SA of our intent to request that Julie's case be presented to the GJ. The SA mentioned they were considering Dangl's plea offer of admitting to employing an unlicensed nurse. I suggested giving them the rest of the week to respond before sending a formal request via certified mail with copies to the media if necessary. Bach agreed and advised that if a plea bargain was accepted, we should attend the hearing and oppose the plea in court, ensuring media coverage.

I responded to Bach with a concern that the SA might accept Dangl's plea, allowing him to avoid jail time. We strongly believe Dangl committed a felony by refusing to approve CPR when Julie flatlined. If this scene were presented to a jury, they would likely find him guilty of felony negligence. A.A. agreed, recommending we write to the SA, stressing that a misdemeanor plea in exchange for our daughter's life is unacceptable. We should demand to be informed of any past and future plea offers to Dangl, keeping a copy for ourselves and considering whether to involve the media.

On October 27, 2006, Maureen and I sent a certified letter to Earl Moreland, the State Attorney for Florida's Twelfth Judicial Circuit, requesting that all evidence in Julie's case be brought before the GJ. We emphasized that accepting a misdemeanor plea for Julie's death is unacceptable, and we are aware that Dr. Dangl has offered to plead guilty to employing an unlicensed nurse. Our main concern is that this plea does not constitute justice, as it allows Dangl to avoid prison time while possibly reinstating his medical license, endangering others. We expressed fear that the SA's office might accept this plea, despite Dangl's gross negligence during Julie's surgery. We reiterated the testimony and facts proving Dangl's malpractice, including expert opinions and witness statements confirming that Julie "flatlined" and was deprived of CPR for five crucial minutes. We requested to be informed of any plea deals and expressed our intent to attend the hearing if a plea was accepted.

On November 3, 2006, we were informed that the sentencing hearing for Lawrence, Dangl's assistant, was delayed until December due to probation violations and attempting to buy drugs illegally.

By November 14, 2006, I learned the Florida Board of Medicine's appeal, supported by the Florida Society of Anesthesiologists, had failed, allowing nurse anesthetists to administer anesthesia in office-based surgeries in Florida.

This highlighted the need for stronger laws governing office-based surgeries, as studies showed higher death rates in such environments compared to hospitals.

In November, I came across a Newsweek review of *Beauty Junkies: Inside Our $15 Billion Obsession with Plastic Surgery* by Alex Kuczynski. Intrigued by its relevance to our efforts, I contacted Kuczynski and discovered that Julie's case was mentioned in the book. This serendipitous discovery led me to purchase the book, where I found Julie's story detailed in a chapter about the dangers of cosmetic surgery. This felt like a significant coincidence, as it aligned with our mission to raise awareness about malpractice in cosmetic surgery.

On November 28, 2006, *The Freeman* in Waukesha reported our opposition to Dr. Dangl's plea deal, and the next day, we were notified by the SA's office that they had reached a settlement with Dangl. He pleaded guilty to employing an unlicensed nurse, a felony, but the deal included dropping his appeal for his medical license and completing community service with probation. The troubling part was that the public wasn't informed of the hearing, preventing us from attending and challenging the plea.

Despite Dangl's felony plea, it seemed the SA's office would allow him to avoid jail time, which felt like an injustice given the criminal negligence surrounding Julie's surgery. His guilty plea to hiring an unlicensed nurse was only tangentially related to the events that led to her death. The failure to prosecute Dangl for his role in Julie's death underscored the lack of legal accountability for medical malpractice in such cases, leaving the medical community to regulate itself.

On December 5, 2006, we were formally notified that Dangl had pleaded guilty, receiving probation, a fine, and a stipulation not to seek a medical license. However, the plea hearing was kept secret, preventing us from appearing in court to contest the deal. Although the media reported Dangl's probation, the coverage inaccurately stated that he pleaded guilty to gross medical negligence, which was not the case, as no such charge was brought against him. This situation highlighted the inadequacy of the legal response to the gross medical negligence that caused our daughter's death.

Chapter Twelve

On December 7, 2006, we marked the anniversary of what's often referred to as "A Date Which Will Live in Infamy"—the attack on Pearl Harbor, which happened 65 years earlier on December 7, 1941. But for us, the Ayer family, we were reflecting on our own escape, which occurred three years prior in 2003.

So, how had we fared since then? Personally, I anticipated Dr. Dangl's bankruptcy, though I thought it would happen a few years earlier. Had the legal system acted on the criminal side of Julie's case, Maureen and I might not have pushed as hard as we did. In the end, the law may have won—or lost, depending on how you look at it. For me, I lost a lot of my drive, the motivation I needed to thrive as a real estate agent. The three months while Julie was still alive felt like everything came to a halt, and afterward, it was just a slow decline. I knew I had lost both momentum and money. This case was so outrageous that I felt compelled to document it. When I was accused of wanting to kill my own daughter, I was overwhelmed with anger. That fury may have been what pushed me to write this. I simply couldn't let Julie's life and death fade away without something positive emerging from it. Maybe, just maybe, a national lawmaker would step up and make a change. I didn't like visiting Julie's grave, but I did it.

As for Maureen, she bounced back from this ordeal better than I did, though she still has a hand tremor that began on the day of our escape. I knew that putting our story into a manuscript sometimes made her uneasy, but she never stopped me, and for that, I'm grateful. Colleen found peace by forgiving, and I believe she found some mental peace. Wade, however, was and probably always will be consumed by rage over Julie's death. The absence of criminal charges related to Julie's surgery, coma, and death left him with a deep anger, which only time might temper.

At the Sarasota County Courthouse, Judge Andrew Owens presided over the sentencing of Lawrence, convicted of probation violations. Lawrence's defense team, including her psychologist and her ex-husband, pleaded for leniency, and she received just a week in jail starting after New Year's, followed by two years of probation. Her life seemed like a wreck, and while I hoped she would find her way, I doubted she would. Despite her marginal involvement in Julie's surgery, we pursued the case because we wanted someone from that clinic to face consequences, even if only for a week. Lawrence was the one who would.

Then, Dr. Kurt Dangl declared bankruptcy. I expected him to appeal to the Florida Department of Health to reinstate his medical license. Around the same time, I came across an article about a teacher, Kelly McGuire, who was fired from her job at a Catholic school after undergoing in vitro fertilization. Despite being a Catholic for most of her life, McGuire lost her job when she became pregnant, with her employers citing violation of Catholic doctrine as the reason. McGuire filed a discrimination complaint based on gender and pregnancy, but the Equal Rights Division upheld her firing. She appealed the decision, but the hearing was delayed. Her attorney argued that the school selectively enforced the employment contract, knowing about the in vitro procedure a month before terminating her after she became pregnant. It felt unfair, especially since McGuire knew men employed by the same school system who had children via in vitro without facing any consequences.

This situation hit close to home because we were once practicing Catholics. When we requested one of our children be confirmed, the parish priest demanded $200—a significant amount for us at the time—so we left the church and never joined another. The Catholic Church's stance on birth control, abortion, and its treatment of women had long disturbed us. Its shielding of child molesters and the antics of conservative Catholics outside the Terri Schiavo hospice added to our frustrations. Watching conservative Republicans and religious figures politicize the Schiavo case was infuriating.

I had just finished reading *Terri, the Truth* by Michael Schiavo and *Using Terri: The Religious Right's Conspiracy to Take Away Our Rights* by Jon Eisenberg. I became convinced that the so-called conservative churches, led by the Catholic Church, had gained a foothold in the Republican Party around the year 2000. It seemed to me that the churches may have even donated campaign money to influence politicians, especially during the Schiavo case. In Eisenberg's book, he tracks millions of dollars flowing to religious groups. This reminded me of our ordeal—though it lasted only 13 weeks compared to the years the Schiavo case dragged on, the parallels were striking.

One of the most telling moments was discovering that,

according to polls, a majority of American Catholics supported the removal of Schiavo's feeding tube, despite the Vatican's opposition. It highlighted how American Catholics often disagree with the official stance of the Church on issues like birth control and abortion, yet remain within the fold. It was fascinating to see people stay loyal to an institution, despite deep disagreements.

Reflecting on all this, I couldn't help but wonder about the legal proceedings. Could a boyfriend of just a few months, engaged for two weeks, hold the legal standing of an "Interested Person" and drag parents of 38 years through eight weeks of court battles? Early on, I asked our attorney, and the answer was simple: Anyone can do it.

Attorney Babette Bach provided the legal definition of an "Interested Person" from Florida Probate Code section F.S. 731.201: an "Interested Person" is anyone who may reasonably be expected to be affected by the outcome of a specific legal proceeding. This definition can vary depending on the individual case and its context. Attorney Bach also mentioned that no case law exists to clarify this definition, so it is ultimately left to the discretion of the judge. This issue arose during our initial hearing, where

Judge Andrew Owens, filling in for Judge Nancy K. Donnellan, ruled that Bonet had standing as an Interested Person. I firmly believe that had Judge Donnellan been present, she might have ruled differently and dismissed Bonet. After Julie's death, I spoke with Judge Donnellan about her interpretation. She had asked several East Coast judges at a judicial conference about the definition, and most agreed that "Interested Person" should apply only to family members. However, with no case law to guide them, there was no definitive answer.

At a lecture given by a law professor who helped draft the statute, I inquired about its interpretation. He admitted they found the definition too difficult to finalize and ultimately abandoned it. This inconsistency created a legal mess. The Florida Probate Rule 5.900, "Expedited Judicial Intervention Concerning Medical Treatment Procedures," allows any adult "Interested Person" to intervene, which, according to a Right to Life advocate, could even include strangers. I hoped the Florida Supreme Court would eventually address this issue.

On December 11, 2006, three years after the traumatic events of December 7, 2003, I reflected on the many injustices we had faced. What should be considered the most egregious? Was it Bonet's actions before he became an official "Interested Person," or the fact that his attorney convinced Judge Owens of Bonet's legal standing? There was also the misleading statement to the press about our family seeking guardianship to remove life support, and Bonet's lawyer's outrageous claim during the hearing that my attitude contributed to Julie's condition.

Other grievances included the so-called Doctor of Chinese Medicine assessing Julie in violation of hospital rules, and the hospital's subsequent inaction. The risk manager's accusations against me for "harassing the nurses" only added to the frustration, as did the hospital's refusal to remove Bonet from the visitation list. There were numerous other incidents: Bonet's proposal to marry Julie while she was in a coma, Julie's handwritten "Do Not Resuscitate" order discovered too late, and the refusal of the state attorney to bring charges against Dr. Dangl. All these incidents were outrageous and added to our distress.

A family friend reviewing the early draft of this account remarked that it seemed like I had "an ax to grind," and he wasn't wrong. Given everything we endured, I feel justified in doing so. I deeply resented being falsely accused of stealing from Bonet's house when we were only searching for Julie's purse, which turned out to be in his safe. I also resented the accusations that we wanted to let our daughter die for financial gain. If we were after money, why would we have returned Julie's engagement ring to Bonet?

Further, Bonet's friends spread malicious rumors, and during the preliminary hearing, Bonet claimed to know Julie better than her own mother. Adding insult to injury, I was asked to sign a document allowing Bonet to marry Julie while she was comatose, supposedly so he could sue the doctor. Meanwhile, Julie's documented wishes about her medical care were withheld from us. The hospital administrators also refused to take action against the Chinese medicine practitioner who evaluated Julie, even though it violated hospital policy.

Our family was also repeatedly threatened with legislative intervention, and the Sarasota State Attorney's Office did not pursue culpable negligence charges. It felt like a double standard, with one set of rules for the wealthy and influential, and another for everyone else.

Wade, my son, shared his thoughts about this ordeal. He

recalled the family's discussions about Julie's wishes and the decision to withhold life support, believing that she would not want to live in a vegetative state. Wade felt Romy, his future wife, provided invaluable support during this difficult time, and their relationship strengthened as a result. He also reflected on how the family's efforts led to increased scrutiny of the Sarasota State Attorney's Office.

Despite documented complaints against Dr. Dangl, the state failed to protect patients like Julie. Wade expressed frustration that it would take further deaths before the Florida Legislature would reform the anesthesia laws. Our family felt a responsibility to push for these changes to ensure that such a tragedy never happens again.

Julie's death resulted from a gross overdose of anesthesia, leading to respiratory arrest. Dr. Dangl administered four to five times the recommended dosage and delayed providing medical aid. I firmly believe this amounts to criminal negligent homicide. Julie had the right to die according to her expressed wishes, but the legal system failed her. We found her written instructions too late, and the courts seemed to prioritize Bonet's brief relationship with Julie over our 38 years as her parents.

The Terri Schiavo case had a profound effect on our family, as we could easily imagine being forced into a similar situation. Julie's death, her wishes, and the legal battle that followed left us with many questions and deep emotional scars.

In October 2003, we all observed Florida's legal system in action. Becoming an "Interested Person" came with significant costs, potentially involving financial obligations for those connected to that person. The legal threshold for becoming an Interested Person seemed quite low—our attorney even remarked, "Anyone can do it." Does that mean any individual or group can qualify? It seems so. What are the criteria in your state, and why aren't there clearer guidelines? It's unsettling.

During Julie's ordeal, Maureen and I were accused of trying to kill our daughter for financial gain. Throughout, Julie's attorney, Sharon O'Day, never intervened because she trusted the medical reports from two neurologists and believed we had accurately communicated Julie's wishes. The entire situation caused enormous damage. Dr. Dangl lost his medical license, was arrested for allowing an unlicensed person to perform medical procedures, and faced possible bankruptcy to avoid a wrongful death lawsuit. That lawsuit remained unresolved. Lawrence also pleaded guilty to practicing medicine without a license, and both Dr. Dangl and Lawrence were placed on probation. Several people were deeply affected, including Bruce Crow, who bravely spoke out about what happened during Julie's surgery. The most devastating loss, however, was Julie's life. On our side, legal defense costs to protect our guardianship rights amounted to around $50,000 over 13 weeks, until Julie passed away on December 26, 2003. I also lost a considerable amount of income during this period. Julie's medical bills exceeded $450,000, and the air ambulance cost $9,000 alone. Her will and trust remained intact, and we made sure that any divorce settlement she received went back to Rubenzer's two daughters.

Bonet's determination to become an Interested Person seemed driven by emotions and rejection of mainstream medical conclusions. When people refuse to accept established medical findings, they often seek alternative opinions. We noticed that some politicians appeared to give equal weight to emotional arguments and expert medical opinions. In Florida, the legislature seemed to avoid criminalizing medical malpractice. As things stand, it appears that states are steering clear of criminal action in such cases, leaving malpractice lawsuits and administrative laws to serve as oversight. This lack of legal enforcement means doctors don't have to worry about criminal prosecution. If these laws don't change, the high mortality rate from cosmetic surgeries will likely persist. One way to address this would be to criminalize level two or level three surgeries performed in doctor's offices, which could reduce the death rate.

During this painful time, Maureen and I couldn't rely on legal remedies, especially given the unpredictability of the lawsuit. After Julie's death, we learned that the State Attorney's Office and the Sarasota County Sheriff's Office had investigated the case. However, it didn't meet the threshold for criminal negligence. We believed Julie's case fell through the cracks. I doubt that the Florida legislature is motivated to create new statutes addressing such cases because they are rare.

Looking at the situation logically, the doctor (who wasn't an anesthesiologist) overdosed Julie with anesthesia. Is that criminal? Apparently not—it's considered ordinary negligence. Julie flatlined on the operating table, and the doctor didn't abandon surgery to attempt resuscitation. Is that criminal? Again, it's deemed ordinary negligence. This "ordinary negligence" feels inadequate, but it's the legal standard.

We later learned that the Florida Department of Health was investigating, starting in November 2003, and that investigation seemed to help. I had tried bringing this issue to the attention of Senator Lisa Carlton but had no success. We still believe there's a gap in the law—one rooted in indifference. The standards for establishing culpable negligence need to be reevaluated. However, fixing this would require concerted efforts from lawmakers or organizations in Florida. One would expect the Florida Prosecuting Attorneys Association (FPAA) to have addressed this issue, but that wasn't the case. Ultimately, this was Florida's problem, not ours, and we could only watch from a distance.

I believe the state of Florida should implement a standard office admission disclosure requiring doctors to provide more detailed information—such as whether they carry malpractice insurance, the presence of recovery systems in their office, and whether the doctor has hospital privileges. Most people, including us, were unaware that not every doctor has hospital privileges. I also lost trust in the Republican Party to represent me or the Silent Majority. Voters, including members of the Silent Majority, are busy with their daily lives and rely on lawmakers to act in their best interest. After the fallout from the Schiavo case, it's unlikely that Republican legislators will repeat such actions in public; future decisions will likely be made behind closed doors.

It's clear that the separation of church and state worked during the Schiavo case, and the Republican Party suffered political damage on that battlefield. Some politicians may have earned figurative "purple hearts," but I doubt they would wear them. Future debates and hearings on the right-to-die cases will likely center around religious and legal questions, but the most effective solution for individuals remains having a written living will. Most people, however, won't create one, just as they often avoid buying life insurance or writing a will—they simply don't want to.

Reflecting on both Julie's case and the Schiavo case, there are many similarities: both women lost oxygen after cardiac events, had no consciousness, and were assessed to be in a persistent vegetative state. Both families faced legal challenges concerning their loved ones' wishes. In both cases, there were medical malpractice or wrongful death suits, autopsies, and cremations. Neither woman had life insurance or a living will, though Julie had a do-not-resuscitate order, which we eventually found. Both families also encountered neurologists who claimed that their loved one wasn't in a vegetative state.

In the end, we were left with emotional and financial scars. Maureen still experienced hand tremors, which an MRI revealed were caused by stress, not disease. Ultimately, we believe Julie's case fell into the cracks between medical malpractice and criminal negligence. A line must be drawn, especially concerning anesthesia levels. Doctors need to be held to a higher standard when administering anesthesia. The cracks in the system must be welded shut to prevent future tragedies.

Three terms haunt me now: anesthesia (especially Propofol), coma, and hyperbaric chamber.

Chapter Thirteen

On March 27, 2007, Maureen and I returned from a 31-day road trip spanning 4,300 miles across the southeastern U.S. One evening, while sitting on the beach with a few drinks, we revisited a question that had been haunting us: why hadn't the state of Florida filed criminal charges in Julie's case? Frustrated and seeking answers, we decided to write a letter to Florida's new attorney general, with a copy to the new governor, requesting them to reopen the investigation. Before sending the letter, we shared a draft with Bruce Crow and attorneys Richard A. "Rich" Filson, Babette Bach, Sharon O'Day, and Amy Boohaker, seeking their feedback.

Bruce Crow's response shocked us. He couldn't believe that Dr. Dangl had Michelle, an unlicensed individual, posing as a nurse during Julie's surgery. He also revealed disturbing details about Dr. Dangl's behavior—throwing tantrums while Julie was in cardiac arrest and violating her privacy by lifting her underwear during the procedure. Crow admitted that, when he gave his recorded statement to the sheriff's office, he left out that Dr. Dangl had actually slid his hand inside Julie's underwear. Crow didn't share this with us initially because he felt we had already been through enough. He also mentioned that during the emergency, there was no proper care being provided to Julie until Michelle arrived to assist, as both he and Amanda thought she was a licensed nurse.

On March 28, 2007, Crow shared more about his visit to the police station. After giving his account of the events at Dangl's office, the officers seemed dismissive, especially when he mentioned the inappropriate behavior. Crow left feeling that his statement wasn't taken seriously. He then decided to visit attorney Robin Guess in Tampa.

Reading Crow's messages deeply disturbed Maureen and me. On April 12, 2007, we sent a letter to the Florida Attorney General in Tallahassee, requesting an independent investigation into Julie's case. Along with the letter, we attached Crow's shocking allegations. We detailed how Dr. Dangl performed a breast augmentation on Julie at his Sarasota office on September 25, 2003. Despite our numerous efforts to bring attention to the case, including formally requesting the State Attorney in Sarasota to present the facts to a grand jury in 2005 (which was denied), no criminal charges had been filed. Everyone—from lawyers to media outlets—continued to ask why the doctor hadn't been held accountable.

In our letter, we outlined several key points of negligence, including how Dr. Dangl had misrepresented the qualifications of the anesthesia provider, administered excessive doses of anesthesia, failed to monitor Julie's vital signs during surgery, and delayed crucial resuscitation efforts after her cardiac arrest. We emphasized that, despite the severity of these failures, the state had consistently dismissed the case. We also included Crow's emails, revealing a potential sexual assault during the surgery, and requested a thorough review of the sheriff's office report. Ultimately, we urged the Attorney General to appoint an independent investigation, with the hope of finally bringing the case to a grand jury.

Despite our efforts, the Attorney General's office referred our letter back to the State Attorney's Office in Sarasota, effectively dismissing our request once again. It was frustrating to see the state of Florida continue to overlook Dr. Dangl's actions during Julie's surgery. At times, I considered turning the email evidence over to the national media but decided to wait until this manuscript was published.

By June 3, 2007, I began contemplating the next steps. Florida had enacted a law in 2000 requiring reports of failed surgeries, enabling the state to track such incidents. However, this system was limited to Florida, and there was no national database for tracking deaths from cosmetic surgeries. While national statistics exist for various causes of death, such as cancer and car accidents, there was no consistent reporting for deaths related to cosmetic surgery. This gap in data collection, whether due to state or national legislation, highlighted a critical issue.

In September 2007, I reflected on the people directly affected by Julie's case and the devastation left in its wake. Larry Bonet, Julie's fiancé at the time, had envisioned a future with her, but her death shattered that dream, leaving him emotionally and financially broken. He even went so far as to challenge my guardianship of Julie's medical decisions, ignoring the opinions of her attending doctors. Then there was Bob Rubenzer, Julie's ex-husband, who faced both emotional and financial devastation after their divorce and her subsequent death. He had witnessed the entire legal aftermath, from malpractice lawsuits to Dr. Dangl's license revocation.

Dr. Dangl himself lost everything—his practice, his license, and his finances due to the legal proceedings. As for Maureen and me, the pain was immeasurable. From the moment we received that first phone call to watching our daughter suffer for months in the hospital, we endured loss after loss. We were forced to relive the trauma during numerous court hearings and legal proceedings, all while trying to piece together what had happened.

The ripple effect of Julie's death impacted everyone involved. It's a grim reminder of the widespread devastation that medical negligence can cause, and the failure of the system to deliver justice has left many of us wondering what could have been done differently to prevent such a tragedy.

Do you think we are still searching for Julie? Maureen mentioned two sightings during the night. Our family has experienced several strange events over the past four years. Personally, I felt compelled to write this book to bring something positive from all of it. What about her sister, Colleen, who visited Sarasota four times in just over two months? Colleen was the sister who used to play with Julie in the playhouse in our backyard. This was the same playhouse where Maureen inscribed the names of our three children and two grandchildren. Are they looking for Julie too? Then there's her brother, Wade, who made one trip to Sarasota the first weekend. He and Julie were incredibly close, and her passing was a deep loss. Wade even had a dream where Julie told him, "Wade, tell Mom and Dad I was just trying to be beautiful." How long will it take him to heal from this? Do you think Wade is searching for Julie?

I believe Bob Rubenzer was the most impacted by this tragedy. What do you think? It was four years ago today, on September 25, 2007, that we received the call from Sarasota. Bonet had said, "They can't wake her up." Despite the time that's passed, the case continues. At that moment, we were locked in a legal battle over whether Dr. Dangl had committed debtor fraud by funneling proceeds from his office building into his homestead. On Julie's estate's behalf, we sought a summary judgment to recover that money. However, Dangl's attorney filed a motion arguing that such action would be unconstitutional in Florida. This created a legal standoff, with conflicting Florida and Federal bankruptcy laws.

On October 11, 2007, it became clear to me after reviewing similar cases that there's a serious problem with cosmetic surgery in this country. The cases in Florida and Arizona seem to represent just a fraction of the issue. There were common trends: surgeries being done in doctors' offices instead of hospitals or accredited surgical centers (ASCs), and a significantly higher death rate in these office-based procedures. Dr. Hector Vilas's study showed a death rate 12 times higher when surgeries were done in a doctor's office. For us, after losing our 38-year-old daughter due to careless and dangerous surgery in a doctor's office under improper anesthesia, I firmly believe that any surgery requiring level three or general anesthesia, if not conducted in an ASC or hospital, should be considered a crime.

Anesthesia providers play a significant role in this problem. When an anesthesiologist administers anesthesia, the death rate is lower, but when a doctor performs surgery and administers anesthesia at the same time, deaths increase. Anesthesiologists refuse to work in doctors' offices—they require proper medical settings like ASCs or hospitals. Moreover, many doctors are trying to pass off level three or general anesthesia as "conscious sedation," but that defense failed during Dr. Dangl's licensing trial.

Another issue is Propofol, a highly dangerous drug when not administered by trained anesthesiologists. It has been involved in too many fatalities. Furthermore, we lack national records on death rates and adverse events related to surgeries, so many needless deaths go unrecorded and unstudied.

Many doctors also operate outside their areas of certification. Surgeons administering anesthesia themselves? That should be criminal. Pre-existing medical conditions are often overlooked, with some patients doctor-shopping to find someone willing to perform risky surgeries.

I suspect that medical malpractice isn't being prosecuted as it should be. I was told by Sarasota's State Attorney's Office that "there's a fine line between malpractice and criminality," but I disagree. It's more like a wall—a wall where the medical license hangs. Practicing without a license is a crime, but practicing outside of one's certification? That's what happened with Julie. The doctor wasn't certified to administer level three anesthesia, but the Florida Board of Medicine (BOM) was left to deal with the sanctions. Given the recklessness in Julie's case, how could it not be considered criminal?

Florida law prohibits someone from maintaining a medical license after being found guilty of three or more incidents of malpractice. I believe that any surgery involving three or more negligent acts that lead to a death should automatically go to a grand jury. Doctors practicing outside their certifications should face the same. Do you think individual states will ever enact such a law? Don't hold your breath. This needs to be addressed at the national level. We need a strong patient safety law and a national reporting system for deaths related to surgery. Doctors must practice within their certification, just like they do in other fields of medicine.

If I ever saw a surgeon practicing anesthesia, I'd hope it would be called Julie's Law. Until then, I ask anyone aware of reckless malpractice resulting in death to contact me. I'd like to investigate whether these cases pass the "sniff test" for further study.

On November 1, 2007, I received a call from our attorneys regarding an arbitration meeting scheduled for November 15th. It seemed urgent. What was the rush? Dr. Dangl was in bankruptcy, so what was left to arbitrate? I wasn't eager to attend and told them I wouldn't go unless my expenses were covered. They assured me expenses would be paid, so I booked a flight to Florida.

There was something else on my mind—deer hunting season in Wisconsin, which started the Saturday before Thanksgiving. I'd been going for over 30 years and didn't want to miss it. So, I meticulously planned my travel: flying from Tampa to Milwaukee, with enough time to get home, grab my gear, and head to camp.

On November 15, 2007, I invited Rubenzer, Julie's ex-husband, to attend the arbitration. After all, his family trust stood to benefit from anything that came out of it. We arrived at the Tampa Airport and met our attorney, Richard Filson. He instructed me to stay quiet and just listen during the meeting. The room was set up with tables arranged in a rectangle. The arbitrator, a retired bankruptcy judge, sat on one side, while Dr. Dangl and his attorney were across from us. Our bankruptcy attorney, Amy Boohaker, was on the other end, with Filson and Rubenzer beside me.

Filson started by making it clear that this arbitration wasn't about money—no amount could replace Julie. The estate was left to Rubenzer's daughters. Then, Dangl's attorney made his statement, and we moved on to our claim for damages. I had little hope for a resolution. After back-and-forth offers, it was clear nothing would be settled.

At one point, the judge asked me if there was anything that could make the arbitration successful. I replied, "You could put him in jail." The judge remarked, "But then you wouldn't get anything." I shot back, "Nothing plus nothing is still nothing."

As expected, the session ended with no resolution. I caught my flight to Atlanta but faced delays when we landed. I was now running late for my connection to Milwaukee. After a long wait and a reroute to Chicago, I finally made it back to Wisconsin by the early hours, just in time for deer camp.

Back in Sarasota, the attorneys didn't rest. Eventually, they reached a settlement, closing Julie's estate after five long years. After expenses, what remained went to Rubenzer's daughters. While it wasn't much, it was better than nothing.

Chapter Fourteen

On April 8, 2008, journalist Bob LaMendola penned an article for the *Ft. Lauderdale Sun Times* detailing an annual disciplinary report from the Federation of State Medical Boards of the United States (FSMB). The report indicated that the state of Florida had taken disciplinary action against 350 medical doctors and 50 osteopathic physicians in the previous year. This marked a significant 25 percent increase from 2002. Officials from the state's health department stated that these figures, made public that Wednesday, were a reflection of their unwavering commitment to patient safety, upheld by the Florida Board of Medicine and the Florida Board of Osteopathic Medicine.

According to Dr. John O. Agwunobi, then Secretary of the Florida Department of Health, the rise in disciplinary actions against doctors did not suggest a decline in the standard of care offered by medical professionals in Florida. Instead, it signified improvements in the procedures for handling medical violations and faster processing times. Out of the 398 actions taken against 380 doctors in 2003, which represented 1.076% of the state's 36,976 practicing physicians, most resulted in licenses being revoked, restricted, or reprimands being issued. This positioned Florida as the leading state in disciplinary actions among those with over 15,000 doctors. Five years prior, Florida ranked 11th nationwide for the number of doctors disciplined and 12th among large states in terms of the percentage of licensed physicians facing disciplinary measures.

After my wife, Maureen, and I uncovered the details of our daughter Julie's tragic death, I predicted that another cosmetic surgery-related fatality would occur in Florida. I feared it would claim the life of another woman and likely take place in a doctor's office, not a certified surgery center, as office-based surgeries carried a higher fatality rate. Sadly, Julie wasn't the first to die following a cosmetic procedure, and, tragically, she wasn't the last. As much as I hate to use these crude terms, the words "next" and "last" capture the cruel reality of this situation. Julie's death was preventable, and knowing that future deaths may follow fills me with grief and frustration.

Unfortunately, cosmetic surgery fatalities aren't isolated incidents. There are too many victims, both known and unknown, going as far back as when cosmetic surgery was first introduced. I want to honor these individuals by recounting a few cases that occurred before Julie's untimely death.

On March 21, 2002, in Hollywood, Florida, a patient undergoing breast augmentation died after receiving an intraoperative *Propofol* infusion for sedation. The drug, which had been prescribed by the surgeon and administered by a registered nurse, led to the patient's complete cardiac arrest. This wasn't an isolated case. Just a few months later, on July 29, 2002, another woman undergoing a facelift in the same city suffered a similar fate. *Propofol* sedation again led to respiratory arrest, anoxic brain injury, and, ultimately, death. Then, on December 18, 2002, a patient in Miami undergoing breast augmentation and liposuction experienced a fatal outcome after being sedated with a combination of *midazolam, fentanyl,* and *Propofol*. This case, like the others, ended in respiratory arrest, an anoxic brain injury, and death a day later.

The chilling part of all this is that Julie became the "next." On September 25, 2003, during her breast augmentation surgery in Sarasota, Florida, Julie was given *Propofol* for sedation. The drug, prescribed by her surgeon and administered by a registered nurse, led to respiratory arrest, an anoxic brain injury, and her eventual death. Her case, unlike many others, garnered national attention.

But she wasn't the last. On April 13, 2004, in Jacksonville, Florida, another patient undergoing liposuction succumbed to respiratory and cardiac arrest just five hours after receiving *Propofol* sedation. Later that same day, in Lakeland, Florida, yet another tragedy occurred. A patient undergoing a photocoagulation/vitrectomy procedure suffered respiratory arrest following multiple *Propofol* boluses for sedation, resulting in an anoxic brain injury and death a week later.

If laws remain unchanged, there will always be another "next." More lives will be lost due to the failures in regulating office-based surgeries. While none of us can completely prevent deaths related to cosmetic surgery, lawmakers and regulatory bodies have the power to reduce the frequency of such tragedies. Whether or not they choose to act remains to be seen.

The article written by LaMendola in 2004 highlighted that Florida was, at least, attempting to address these issues.

However, the broader picture remained grim. In this book, I have repeatedly emphasized the need for change. I wasn't alone in calling for action, but the question remains—how do we achieve it? In an ideal world, a national standard would supersede the individual states, many of which have no laws prohibiting office-based surgeries. I didn't know which states had such laws and which didn't. But I knew one thing: the medical community cared deeply, while the legal and political systems did not.

Determined to explore any avenue for change, I sent letters to Wisconsin Senators Russell Feingold and Herb Kohl. I described the dire situation in hopes of getting their attention. Unfortunately, my efforts were fruitless. Senator Feingold's office at least responded, though predictably, there was no interest in addressing the issue. I also reached out to the medical correspondent at CNN and even to Senator Edward Kennedy's office, but again, I was met with silence. The Center for Disease Control (CDC), too, was powerless, as they didn't have the authority to prosecute. The Florida district attorneys were equally indifferent.

By April 28, 2008, it became clear to me why there was such a widespread lack of concern. The indifference stemmed from the way medical malpractice lawsuits are handled in this country. These cases are often drawn out over years, diluting the emotional weight of the incident and draining the resources of the plaintiff. Most of the time, these cases never reach a trial jury; instead, they are quietly settled with confidentiality agreements, which keeps the public in the dark. It's a secretive system, and those involved seem content to maintain that secrecy.

I also struggled to get other families to share their stories for this book. Their reluctance was understandable—many of these cases were hidden from the public eye, never reported to any central system. I wondered, would requiring mandatory reporting of medical malpractice cases change anything? Would it bring these hidden cases into the light and force people to pay attention?

The sad reality is that cosmetic surgery is often dismissed as frivolous, even by me at times. Julie's surgery was no different, and society as a whole views these procedures with a level of indifference. Lawmakers and prosecutors don't see the need to address an issue that most people don't seem to care about. The state attorney's office in Sarasota certainly didn't, and if they wouldn't prosecute a case like Julie's, then no medical malpractice case is likely to receive the justice it deserves. The shield of a medical license protects practitioners, no matter how severe their negligence.

And so, the question remains—who's next? As I write this, there are men and women, mostly women, walking on beaches, contemplating cosmetic surgery. Each one of them could be the next victim. The first "next," the second "next," and so on, stretching into perpetuity. There will always be another "next." I only hope that by sharing Julie's story, I can help reduce the number of deaths.

The only cases that seem to capture public attention are those involving celebrities, but if you're not a star, your death will likely go unnoticed by the national media. And if you haven't completed a living will, your family may be the next to enter the courthouse, fighting a legal battle for a loved one's life.

By September 9, 2008, I realized that I hadn't learned anything new that I didn't already know. The CDC confirmed in writing that there wasn't a national mandatory reporting system. On October 14, Maureen and I wrote a letter to our attorney, Rich Filson, thanking him for his dedication to Julie's case. Filson had promised not to give up, and he stayed true to his word, even though there was no financial reward for him. We knew that Julie's case was never about money for him, just as it wasn't for us.

On October 15, I received an email from Amy Boohaker, acknowledging Filson's efforts and praising him for embodying the best of the legal profession. She recognized that Filson had done the moral and just thing, even when there was no monetary gain in it for him. In response, I thanked her and shared a memory from five years prior when Maureen, our daughter Colleen, and I were in court, defending myself against the absurd accusation that I had tried to kill Julie. Babette, our attorney at the time, had held off those baseless claims.

On October 17, Filson wrote to us again, reminding us that we too had persevered throughout the case. He acknowledged that even a billion dollars in insurance wouldn't have been enough to compensate us for the loss of our daughter. Though his file on Julie's case was closed, he assured us that if Dr. Dangl failed to meet his financial obligations as outlined in the settlement agreement, he would take action to ensure justice was served.

In this journey, we've learned that while the system may

be stacked against us, there are still individuals, like Filson, who are willing to fight for what's right. The road to justice for Julie has been long and difficult, but we remain committed to seeing it through.

And yet, the question remains: who's next? Despite the progress we've made in holding some individuals accountable, I know there are more lives at risk. The system, as it stands, isn't equipped to prevent future tragedies like Julie's. It's clear that cosmetic surgery, especially when conducted in office-based settings, poses significant risks that are often downplayed or overlooked.

The system failed Julie, just as it has failed many others. The legal, political, and medical communities continue to treat cosmetic surgery fatalities as isolated incidents or unfortunate accidents, rather than as systemic failures that demand reform. The lack of a national standard for reporting medical malpractice, particularly in cosmetic surgery, means that these deaths go largely unnoticed by the public and unpunished by the courts. And as long as the general public remains unaware of the true dangers, and as long as lawmakers refuse to address the issue, the cycle will continue.

When Maureen and I sat in court, fighting for justice for our daughter, it became clear that we were not just battling the individuals who had failed Julie, but a system designed to protect its own. Doctors and medical professionals are given an enormous amount of trust, and while many of them uphold their oaths to "do no harm," there are those who operate negligently, shielded by their medical licenses. The fact that someone like Dr. Dangl could continue practicing despite his history is a testament to how flawed the system is.

What's perhaps most infuriating is the indifference. When a high-profile case emerges, the media might cover it for a short while, but the attention is fleeting. Politicians might express concern, but then move on to the next issue. Families like ours are left to pick up the pieces, while the medical community continues with business as usual. The truth is, unless a case garners national attention, it's swept under the rug. But for every high-profile case, there are countless others that go unreported, unseen, and unaddressed. These are the "Nexts" I fear for.

After Julie's death, we made a commitment to try and make a difference—to prevent other families from experiencing the same heartbreak. But it hasn't been easy. The responses from lawmakers and legal authorities have been tepid at best. My letters to Senators Feingold and Kohl, to CNN's medical correspondent, and even to Senator Edward Kennedy's office, all went unanswered. The silence was deafening. Even the CDC, the very organization that should be collecting and analyzing data on these deaths, lacks a mandatory reporting system.

Without transparency, there is no accountability. When cases are quietly settled with confidentiality agreements, the public remains in the dark. These settlements may provide financial compensation to grieving families, but they don't bring about real change. They don't prevent the next death, the next tragedy, the next family left shattered.

The medical community, as I've said before, does care about these issues. There are doctors and healthcare professionals who see the need for reform and are willing to fight for it. But their voices are often drowned out by a system more focused on protecting its own interests than protecting patients.

The legal system, on the other hand, has shown little interest in pursuing justice for victims of medical negligence in cosmetic surgery cases. If the state attorney's office in Sarasota refused to prosecute Julie's case, it's hard to imagine they'd prosecute any similar case. This unwillingness to hold negligent doctors accountable sends a dangerous message: as long as you have a medical license, you're above the law.

For years, Maureen and I have worked to bring attention to these issues. We've written letters, spoken out, and tried to connect with other families who have lost loved ones to cosmetic surgery. Some have been willing to share their stories, but many are hesitant, fearful of retribution or simply too overwhelmed by their grief. But their silence only serves to perpetuate the problem.

If more people were aware of the true risks of cosmetic surgery, particularly in office-based settings, perhaps they would think twice before going under the knife. Perhaps they would demand better regulations, better oversight, and better accountability. But as it stands, the secrecy surrounding these cases allows the cycle to continue. Doctors like the ones responsible for Julie's death can continue practicing with little fear of repercussions.

It's been over five years since Julie died, and in that time, we've seen little progress in terms of legal or medical reforms. While we did achieve a legal settlement in Julie's case, it was never about the money for us. It was about justice—justice for Julie, and for all the other victims who came before her and after her. We wanted to ensure that no other family would have to endure the pain and heartbreak that we have. But the truth is, as long as the system remains unchanged, there will always be another family, another victim, another "Next."

We all wrestled with feelings of guilt and anger—guilt for not being able to protect Julie, and anger at those who failed her. But I've come to realize that my anger, while justified, isn't enough to bring about change. I've had to forgive myself for the things I couldn't control, and focus on what I can do moving forward.

Maureen and I will continue to fight for change, even if the progress is slow and the obstacles seem insurmountable. We owe it to Julie, and to all the other victims whose names we may never know. I don't want another family to go through what we have, to lose a loved one to something as preventable as a botched cosmetic surgery. The laws need to change. The medical community needs to be held accountable. And the public needs to be informed about the real dangers of these procedures.

There will always be another "Next," but maybe, just maybe, through our efforts and the efforts of others, we can reduce the number of lives lost. We can't bring Julie back, but we can honor her memory by fighting for the changes that should have been in place long ago. This battle isn't just for her—it's for all the future "Nexts" who deserve better.

We can't afford to remain silent any longer. It's time for real action, real reform, and real justice for those who have been failed by the system. Until that happens, we will continue to ask the question: who's next? And we will continue to fight for those who deserve answers, accountability, and most importantly, safety.

Conclusion

I reflect on the painful journey we endured, a journey that could have taken an even darker turn had we not made a critical decision at the last moment. On Sunday, December 7, 2003, we secretly switched Julie's ambulance flight from Monday to Sunday, a move that spared us from becoming entangled in a prolonged legal battle that would have mirrored the Terri Schiavo case. I call this day "The Second Day of Infamy," drawing a parallel to Pearl Harbor, as it marked a pivotal moment where we narrowly avoided a nightmare scenario.

Had we not acted, Bonet's lawyer, Bob Jackson, was already plotting to involve the Florida legislature, intending to force us to return Julie to Florida. The consequences would have been disastrous. I can still visualize the Florida State Police being ordered to block Julie's departure from the hospital, trapping us in endless legal motions and financial ruin, forcing us to leave Julie behind.

I believe that had we not acted, Bonet and Jackson would have seized guardianship, making Julie a "ward" of the state. But we outmaneuvered them, escaping what could have been a Florida version of the Schiavo case by just one day.

For the past two decades, I have wondered why Governor Jeb Bush and other key players took the bait and were so quick to intervene in similar cases. Jon Eisenberg's book, Using Terri, provides the answer: political manipulation by the Religious Right. I often wonder what these Florida officials would say today if confronted with their actions in front of the media.

This experience serves as a wake-up call. When this story is fully told, I plan to create a platform, "The Julie Rubenzer Society," where people can share their own experiences with elective or cosmetic surgeries. This will be a space for those who bypassed their regular physicians, went to unregulated clinics, and faced the dangers of surgeries performed without proper safeguards. Our story isn't just about Julie—it's about the systemic flaws in healthcare and the legal system that allowed this tragedy to happen.

In the end, I'll write a follow-up book, drawing from the stories of others, making sure Julie's legacy serves as a warning and a call for change. This journey has not only been about loss but also about ensuring no other family has to go through what we did.

www.ingramcontent.com/pod-product-compliance
Lightning Source LLC
Chambersburg PA
CBHW051613120626
46551CB00014B/1773